DISCARDED

I'm So Glad You Found Me in Here

by
Matthew Hobson and Nancy Hobson

Ithaca Press
3 Kimberly Drive, Suite B
Dryden, New York 13053 USA
www.IthacaPress.com

Cover Design Gary Hoffman
Book Design Gary Hoffman

Manufactured in the United States of America

9 8 7 6 5 4 3 2 1

Library of Congress Cataloging-in-Data Available

First Edition

Printed in the United States of America

ISBN 978-0-9819746-9-9

www.HobsonBooks.com

This book is dedicated to my grandma
who helped lead me to Laura Poorman.

Acknowledgments

I would like to thank all of those people who have supported and encouraged me. Each of you has made my life better by believing in me. I thank my family and all of our friends. Thank you, Stephanie and Josh for your care and for your friendship. I want to thank my many teachers, bus drivers, and school personnel who dealt with my autism. Many thanks to Kriss and Carla for toughing out the hard times and sticking with me. I also appreciate Evalyn Kellum's hard work in helping provide the funding for my facilitators in college. A special thank you to my dad and mom for not giving up on me. Thanks to Joey, Katy and Melissa who I dearly love. I also thank Joan Mayor and Maddy Walsh for making this book a reality.

Foreword

I first met Matthew Hobson on paper. He was no more than a concept that was slipped into my mailbox at school. Words like "non-verbal", "autistic", "facilitated communication" and "non-intentional auditory disruptions" filled the page like an insincere apology. It was the second semester of my first year teaching. I was fresh out of school myself, and I was not looking forward to having a student placed into my class who I felt I had no business teaching.

When I met Matt, I was even more terrified. He rocked back and forth like someone who wants to get up but is unable to commit. He occasionally drooled and moaned half audible words that didn't seem to connect to any greater theme or purpose. This "broken" child was supposed to take and pass a high school level speech course? "Typical," I thought. Typical of a school system that no longer works. Toss these kids into mainstream classes, and pretend like you're making progress.

I'm couldn't have been any more wrong about Matt and the system that placed him into my classroom.

The days turned into weeks, and I as I watched Matt at his desk, I began to see a bright young man who wasn't simply a mess of physical tics and verbal babble. For me, the realization didn't come during some definitive moment or after some amazing conversation I had with him. Day by day I learned to shut off my impatient and selfish thoughts and listen to Matthew; I learned to slow down, and I don't mean that in any intellectual sense but that I learned to curb my impatience and see the world through his eyes. It was sobering to have a young man with such serious challenges to his communicative abilities teach me how to honestly and unabashedly listen.

Together Matt and I began to forge an educational relationship. I let go of my preconceived notions of his abilities, and he helped me create a way for him to benefit from a class on public speaking. As a team we approached the obstacles from a sociological standpoint. In each speech Matt wrote, he included in his footnotes both the mechanisms of presentation and tactics for success of the objective. I would then present his speech for him. There were highs and lows, but we always moved forward. There is no doubt that I became better at teaching speech to all students because of Matthew. Matt also took my drama class, and he wrote one of the most emotionally charged pieces of theatre I've ever been privileged to be a part of as an actor, teacher or director.

When I first met Matt I experienced pity and fear, but to know Matt is not to pity him for his condition or to fear him for his outward carriage. To truly know Matt is to know strength of character, patience, and unwavering honesty.

I can say that my experiences with Matthew will live with me until I'm no longer on this earth. I've learned more from Matt than I could have ever taught as a teacher. I am thankful for his patience with me and for his gentle soul that helped me along the way.

Michael T. Downey
May, 2010

Prologue

This book is a gift of hope to the parents of a child with special needs. Wanting normal, healthy children is the prayer of most expecting mothers. Most babies come into the world just like that. However, sometimes God has a different purpose. Those children come to this world with many obstacles. I know, because I am one of them. I hope to encourage parents to strive to give their child every chance to reach his or her potential. This book could only be written due to the facilitated communication that my mother helped me learn. The encouragement I received changed my life. A normal child can benefit from encouragement, but the special needs child can only thrive with much help and constant searching for a way to make life better. This search led my mother to a lady named Laura

Poorman who saved my life. She discovered a good mind inside a disabled human being. As a result, I am able to write my story. I feel that if reading my experiences helps one child, this book will be a success.

Not Like It Seems

By Katy Hobson

If this leaf could talk
It would tell a person
About his hopes and dreams
That he's not like he seems
If this leaf could talk
He would speak of autism
And all he's gone through
Times that made him happy, times that made him blue
If this leaf could talk
He would tell of the day everything changed
The day we realized his intelligence and all he knew
That he was in there all along, too
If this leaf could talk
He would mention a friend
A friend that someone would never be
If only they would get to know him, they would really see
If this leaf could talk
His world would be so much better
He would burst and bubble with glee
Like a small child telling an exciting story
If this leaf, my brother, could talk
He would share his adventures and obstacles
His hopes and his dreams
He's not really what he seems

Introduction

The dream of my life had come true. It was finally graduation night. I sat there in my purple cap and gown, ready to receive my high school diploma. Was the moment really here? I knew my parents were sitting in the bleachers thinking the exact same thing. None of us expected in a million years that this would be a possibility. Not only was I graduating, but the other tremendous thing was that I had been accepted at Indiana University Purdue University of Indianapolis, a nearby college.

The difference in my graduation, from other students, was that until I was eleven years old, I was diagnosed as severely mentally handicapped. The only classes I had been in, at

that point, were segregated special education classes. The other difference was that I was totally nonverbal. For the first eleven years of my life, graduating from high school was a thing that was suspended in the air, dangling there for others, but not for me. Until the day I met Laura Poorman...

CHAPTER 1

Disbelief, Anger and Fear

Sitting in a rocking chair at Riley Children's Hospital, I wanted to pinch myself. I was living a nightmare. I just couldn't believe it was me sitting there, rocking my "abnormal" baby. In the last few days, we had discovered that our son Matthew had all kinds of problems.

When I was three to four months along with my pregnancy, the OB/GYN had sent me for an ultrasound. I was a bit bigger than I should have been at that point in my pregnancy. The doctor thought there was a possibility that I might be carrying twins. During the ultrasound we could not see my baby's arms. This worried me to no end. My doctor assured me, though, that he would have arms, and that I could shake hands with him in about five months. And he was right. Matthew was born, after being induced, on March 30, 1982. As we watched a space shuttle landing on television, Matt made his appearance. The doctor, however, did not make his appearance at the hospital in time. My husband Mel held one leg, and a fireman, updating his training, held the other as a resident delivered Matt. He had all of his body parts, to my relief.

But as I look back, I knew from the beginning that something was different. When the nurses brought Matthew to me in the hospital, he wasn't crying. He had to have been hungry and should have been crying like the other babies. He just rested in my arms and waited patiently to be nursed. At home he would lie on the couch and look at the corners of the big picture window in our living room. He seemed to be fascinated with the corners of windows and doorframes. Another clue that something was different was that when he nursed, milk would run down his chin. It would be a mess. I just blamed myself for having too much milk. There were other things that didn't seem normal. The day we brought him home from the hospital he only slept about ten minutes at a time, and that would be after rocking him forty to forty-five minutes. He would get so tired that he would have dark circles under his eyes when he was only three months old. Matthew started crying all of the time. Sure, no big deal – it was just a bad case of colic according to the doctor. Mel and I would rock him, and he would grab at our necks, pinching our skin. We had to hold his arms under ours and hold his legs with our hands to keep him still so that he would eventually fall asleep. I would call my mom crying, and she would come over to relieve me because I thought I couldn't do it another day. We lived out on the front porch swing because the swaying seemed to calm Matthew.

It was a horrible time, but it was going to get worse. Much worse. During several office visits, the pediatrician reassured me that things were fine; I was just comparing him too much to Joey, our older son by four years. There was no doubt that Joey had achieved most developmental milestones early, but in my heart, I just knew that something wasn't right with Matthew. At seven months when he was still not supporting his head very well and not even close to sitting up, the doctor referred us to a well-known pediatric neurologist. I left school early, where I was teaching third grade, to go with my husband and seven-month-old Matthew to the neurologist. We sat in the waiting room nervously awaiting the truth. I had dressed Matt in his little red shirt and railroad overalls. I wanted him to look so cute. Finally, after what seemed an eternity, this bald man with black horn rim glasses escorted us to an exam room. He took Matt from us and moved him this way and that. He said very little. He took Matt's clothes off down to his diaper. I remember carefully folding each item of clothing as he handed it to me. Finally, he said that our son definitely had problems, developmental delays. As he talked to us, he would glance up at me and stare. He would ask, "How does this make you feel?" As

Mel and I sat with tears rolling down our cheeks, I just wanted to scream at him, "How in the hell do you suppose it makes me feel?" As I remember, I just stared back at him in disbelief.

Then the doctor had us go with him down the hall and into a small bathroom. He closed the door and did not turn on the lights. We stood in the dark holding our baby, wondering what in the world we were doing. Then he turned on a flashlight and looked at Matthew's skull. He said that he was looking to see if there was water on the brain. This was the strangest doctor I had ever met, and I hated him. I truly hated him – his bald head, his black rim glasses, his weird bedside manner and the horrible news that he had given us.

He told us to take Matthew to a pediatric ophthalmologist for an eye exam. He wasn't sure if he could really see or hear normally either. We took Matt and put him in his car seat in my sporty, red Firebird. I loved that car. But now thinking about it brings back horrible memories. We went straight to my mom and dad's house. They were keeping Joey for us while we had had our appointment. I remember going up the two stairs into the kitchen and telling them the bad news: "Our baby has a lot of problems." My mom took Matt from me and clutched him to her chest. We all cried as Mel and I shared what the doctor had told us. All of my fears and worries had come true.

When we got home, I had to go for a walk to get some fresh air. I walked for a while and then stopped at our next door neighbor's house. He was sitting out on the porch. His son had Down's Syndrome. I just felt like talking to him was the thing to do. I knew he had experienced some of the pain that I was now feeling. We talked for a while, and he consoled me. What else could I expect? Nothing was really going to help. That evening I called our minister, but I didn't know him well. Again, I got kind words but no sense of relief for the heart crushing pain I was experiencing.

A day or two later we took Matt to a pediatric ophthalmologist at Riley Hospital. We sat in a huge waiting room filled with small children for a couple of hours. At one point I went to the restroom down the hall. As I was returning to the waiting room, a poem on the bulletin board caught my eye. It was the first sense of emotional relief I had felt. It read:

Heaven's Very Special child

A meeting was held quite far from earth,
It's time again for another birth.
Said the angels to the Lord above,
This special child will need much love.
His progress may seem very slow,
Accomplishments he may not show
And he'll require extra care
From the folks he meets way down there.
He may not run or laugh or play:
His thoughts may seem quite far away.
In many ways he won't adapt,
So he'll be known as handicapped.

So let's be careful where he's sent.
We want his life to be content.
Please Lord find parents who
Will do a special job for you.
They will not realize right away
The leading role they're asked to play
but with this child sent from above,
Comes stronger faith and richer love.
And soon they'll know the privilege given
In caring for this gift from heaven.
Their precious charge, so meek and mild
Is heaven's very special child.
(author unknown)

A friend gave me a copy of it on a plaque that I hung in my bedroom. I still read it often. How true: "They will not realize right away the leading role they're asked to play." At the time I first read it, I had no idea how important our role would be in Matthew's life.

Again the eye doctor had more bad news. He did not know how well Matthew was seeing because he would not track objects with his eyes. He had a little board with chickens that pecked. Matthew couldn't have cared less about it. He recommended that we let him put Matt to sleep and look into his eyes for a thorough exam, so we combined a cat scan of his brain and the eye exam into one appointment. I sat in the rocking chair, rocking my baby in front of a window looking out over the medical center. It had only been a few days since visiting the neurologist, but like most nightmares, it seemed an eternity. Matt's optic nerve was underdeveloped but was functioning and the doctor assured us that he could see, and that the cat scan of his brain was normal. That was the first positive news we had had yet.

CHAPTER 2

Blaming Myself

The next few weeks were foggy. I was going through the daily life experiences but felt like I was in someone else's body. I would go to school, but no one really knew the extent of what I was experiencing. People would come up and offer consoling words. Sometimes I smiled and thanked them. Other times my eyes filled with tears. I was such a mess. I was so angry with God. I just couldn't understand what I had done to deserve this. I had prayed every night of my pregnancy for a normal, healthy baby. I had tried to do everything right. I started searching for answers.

We had Matt's hearing checked, and we visited several different neurologists and specialists in the field. They all painted the same bleak story. They all said, "Take him home and love him." After these visits I would go home and think and think about what I could have done wrong during my pregnancy to have caused this abnormality. At first I blamed it on the wasp spray the custodians had used in my room at school. The odor lingered a few days, and I became certain that that was the cause of Matthew's problems. I just couldn't imagine why God had let me down. I had prayed so hard during my pregnancy and tried to do everything just right. I felt as if I was being punished for something I must have done. Once in the middle of the night, I awoke with a start and cried to Mel, "I know what did this!" One night during my pregnancy I had fallen asleep with the electric blanket on high. I knew it was that extra warmth that had caused my baby to be handicapped. It was all my fault. I went for weeks wondering how I was going to live with myself.

I had never really known anyone well who had a child with any disabilities. My mother's beautician had a son with a mental handicap. I had been around him a few times. My neighbor's son was more of an adult when I met him. I just had no one to connect with or talk to. I desperately felt the need to talk to someone, anyone, who had gone through this. There was a second grade teacher in my building who had a son with "problems." I always thought she was kind of grumpy and standoffish. Now I was beginning to see maybe why she was the way she was. As time went on, it turned out that she was the one person I could talk to. She proved to be a wonderful support.

Every time I saw another baby, I felt like my heart was going to break. This baby or that baby had a chance and mine didn't. I resented mothers who were pregnant and smoking, eating junk food, or just looked like they weren't taking care of themselves. I knew they would probably have a normal, healthy baby, and at that time, I thought they didn't deserve one. And I knew I did.

Near the end of that month, Mel's family had a get-together at a restaurant in one of the state parks. I honestly did not know how I was going to face everyone for the first time since we had gotten all of this news about Matthew. I remember at that time I felt like I would never smile again or be truly happy. I dreaded going. When we got to the restaurant, I don't remember much of what was said. I just remember that after we had eaten our dinner, we went downstairs to a game room. There was ping-pong and some arcade games. Mel's sister and I started playing this racing game. We were controlling these little cars as they went around a track on the screen. We constantly rammed into each other as we tried our best to maneuver them to the finish line. No matter how hard we tried, we kept crashing into one another to the sound of grinding metal. I started laughing and couldn't stop. I laughed so hard, I cried. It felt so good to laugh again. I will never forget that day. Going to that restaurant was the best thing I could have done. I knew then that life *would* go on.

CHAPTER 3

Light at the End of the Tunnel

When we went back to the neurologist for the second visit, he suggested that we get Matthew into Riley Hospital for physical and occupational therapy. We took Joey with us and met with two therapists after school one day. These young women became our light at the end of the tunnel. I told the physical therapist that if we could get Matt to sit up, I felt like he would also walk someday. She agreed and gave us the first ray of hope. A triangle of muscles that should appear in a baby's back had not developed in Matt's. She sent us home with a list of exercises to do with him that would strengthen those muscles. We started that night and did them religiously. Joey was right there, encouraging his little brother to work hard. I was worried about Joey and how Matthew's problems would affect him. However, one day while I was working with Matthew on some of his exercises, Joey was sitting beside me staring at Matt. Joey put my mind at ease when he quietly said, "Matt's a good brother for me – maybe not for everybody, but he is a good brother for me."

Going to school was very difficult for me. I later read that discovering your child is disabled is like going through a death in the family – the death of your prayer for a normal, healthy child. However, no one really knew or understood the heartache we were going through. When a person suffers a loss due to the death of a family member, it is a moment in time. People understand your pain and can empathize with that loss. But this was different. My husband and I had suffered a terrible heartache, but it was not going to get easier with the passing of time. Time was not going to heal this ache.

The hardest part of school was looking at my class and the other classes of children. Everywhere I looked, I saw all of those normal, healthy children. Why, oh why, couldn't my baby be like that? Even looking at the pictures in my students' phonics books of a tricycle or a bat and ball caused sadness, and I would have to turn away from my students to compose myself.

We had to take Matthew to physical and occupational therapy every other week. I had to leave school a half hour early to make the therapist's last appointment. My principal was so kind. He let me take his lunch duty, and he took my class the last thirty minutes on the days we had appointments. I lived for those visits. Every time we went, his therapists could see a difference. Soon the little triangle of muscles became apparent in his back. He started supporting his head and was on the verge of sitting alone. Finally, at eleven months, he did sit alone. It seemed like it took forever, but it was a ray of hope.

Every time Matthew did something new, I called my mom and dad and all of my friends. The first time he picked up his cup from his high chair tray was monumental. After months of exercises, Matt began to crawl, pull up, and then even walked at the age of eighteen months. Therapy at Riley had seemed to work miracles for a while. We saw such progress.

We worked with those two therapists until Matthew was five years old. I was disappointed when they told us they had reached the limit of how much help they could provide for him. Those visits were what had gotten me through each week. Now I wasn't going to have them.

Matthew also went to Riley's Children Hospital for two different eye surgeries. His eyes were still crossing and had to be straightened. The doctors and nurses were absolutely wonderful. Staying several days and a couple of nights at the hospital made me realize how much worse it could be. I saw so many sick and deformed children. I felt lucky that we didn't have worse problems.

CHAPTER 4

Entering the Educational System

I can't begin to explain how quiet you feel when the rest of the world speaks. I know only too well. I have lived in silence. I have gotten used to it, having never had the opportunity to speak. It is very lonely much of the time. People talk to me, but I have no way to respond. I want to have the chance to open my mouth to just talk like the rest of the world does, but nothing happens. I know the words I want to say but nothing seems to work. My tongue and my lips will not form the words I wish to speak. My body will not cooperate with my mind.

Even though I have learned to deal with this disability, the world is a strange and scary place. I have no gift of speaking to protect my family or myself. I have no way of shouting or telling them that I need help or that they might be in danger. The world is a frightening place to live in when you have no ability to help yourself. It really took me a long time to understand why I could not talk like the people around me. The inability to communicate my thoughts or feelings has left me alone to find my own quiet place in a world over which I have no control.

I think that speech is the most important thing that children develop. It changes their inability to communicate as infants into a powerful force, not only allowing them to achieve their wants and needs, but to do so much more. The ability to speak actually opens up the world. You can say what things you like or dislike. You can explain the feelings you have. You can talk about your day. You can tell your parents that you feel sick or that something hurts. One time I got my finger caught in the car door. My parents didn't realize it. The next day it was swollen and bruised. They felt terrible because I couldn't tell them that it was broken or how badly it hurt.

I do not cry and do not show many emotions. Also, I do not point to things. My brain won't let me, but I don't know why. I had hoped

and prayed that someday my brain would give me the ability to verbalize my thoughts, feelings and needs, but it never happened. When I was young I used to sit in the sink in front of the mirror in my parents' bedroom. I would look in the mirror to watch my mouth move as I tried to form the words I wanted to say, but I only made the sound of random letters. I wanted to cry out for help so badly, but I couldn't. I wanted to join in conversations as I grew older. I wanted to have a part in family decisions. The worst thing was not having the ability to tell my parents that I loved them.

I remember the frustration I felt when people did not think I knew anything. But I did know a lot. I knew more than they ever would have thought possible. Like most kids, I knew colors, numbers, letters and other common things. I even knew how some words looked. Some words I knew from TV like Wheel of Fortune. I probably learned the most from seeing Sesame Street at my babysitter's house. This was such a disturbing time in my life. The saddest thing was that I knew so much but didn't have a chance to share it with anyone.

The real gift of communication didn't come until much later. That method has helped but never has replaced the very necessary feat of verbally speaking.

When I was three years old, I started going to Noble Preschool. It was for kids with handicaps, and it was good. The best thing was Dana Green, my teacher when I was five. She believed I could do things. She wanted to help me find a way to communicate but nothing worked. I liked Noble but would have rather been at Nina's house with the regular kids. Nina was my babysitter. I especially had fun at Nina's because my baby sister went with me. It was good for me to go to Noble Preschool though.

As a child, the usual toys did not interest me. The thing that I found most fascinating was angles. I really enjoyed looking at angles formed in the corners of doors and windows. The realization that they made shapes kept my fascination going. I also spent time staring at a light in the refrigerator. The shining light bulb intrigued me. This upset my parents. One time I got into the chocolate syrup and dumped it all over our new carpet. That was just the tip of the iceberg. I did a lot of things that upset them.

When Matthew was two, doctors recommended that we send him to a developmental preschool. We started investigating and found that since we lived in Hendricks County, we had to send him to a school called Opportunity Cottage in Danville, a nearby town in the same county. But the other teacher at the school where I taught, who had a son with a mental handicap, suggested I call Noble Preschool in Indianapolis. Her son had gone there many years before, and she felt that it was a wonderful school. That was the beginning of my first real battle. I had always been the shy, quiet type for the most part, but I was soon to learn that I had a whole different me inside. If Noble was the best preschool for Matthew, Mel and I made up our minds that he should go there, regardless of what county we lived in. I called Noble Preschool and talked to the director. He was very nice and encouraging but was not sure if Matt would be able to go there. In Brownsburg I found another parent who had fought for her son to go to Noble. She suggested I call the governor's office. Day after day I made phone calls to various people, insisting, pleading, questioning and doing whatever it took. My principal again helped me out. He would let me use the only private phone in the building, the one in his office, during my prep times to make my phone calls.

The director of Opportunity Cottage invited us to come and see her school. She thought that a visit would relieve our anxiety about sending Matthew there. It was a late afternoon in the winter when we looked around the facility and listened to her explain the program. I will never forget that evening – it was dark outside and gloomy inside. We sat around the table with the director. She pushed the papers in front of Mel and me, and said, "Here's where you sign." I felt as if we were being shanghaied. There was no way we were going to sign those papers that evening, but we were told that we really had no other choice.

After weeks and weeks of battling, (the governor's receptionist now knew and recognized my voice), we got a call from the director at Noble. Matthew was accepted! We had to provide the transportation, but he could come. Mel and I were ecstatic. All of the time, work, calls and resistance had been worth it. Now if they could only help our son.

Noble Preschool was in Indianapolis, about thirty minutes from our home. Mel, who was working for himself at the time, took Matt every morning. On his first day I fought back the tears throughout the hours. When Mel brought him home, there was the nicest note from his teacher. I still have it. It reassured me that we had done the right thing fighting to send him to Noble. It seemed each day she found something positive to say. Even though there were no miracles or great gains, just knowing that our son was with such kind, knowledgeable people gave us hope. At first Matthew went every day, but we soon realized it was just too physically tiring for him, so we cut back to three days a week. The other two days he went back to the babysitter's house. I was happy that there he was surrounded by typically developing children. They were wonderful models for Matt, and his babysitter, Nina, was the dearest grandmotherly woman. She loved Matthew and constantly did everything she could to help him, including all of the exercises his therapists showed us to do with him.

CHAPTER 5

Another Evaluation

When Matthew was three or four years old, we had him evaluated by a lady who was considered the "queen of autism." She was so nice to talk to. She did a battery of tests with Matt, though not in our presence, of course. Testing is rarely, if ever, done in the parents' presence. After a couple of weeks, she compiled the results and shared them with us. Of course, Matthew did not do well on the tests. He could not speak, did not point, and could not really manipulate objects in a meaningful way. She told us, "Based on all available evidence, Matthew is severely retarded." She reported that he did have one strength: his appearance. He was cute – very handsome, in fact. Well, that was a real hope-booster! I was always glad he was physically "cute," but was that going to get him by in life? Not hardly. It was a very disappointing summary of our child's strengths and weaknesses. He was very passive and had low muscle tone, but at least he was cute. The specialist provided little information that would guide us in helping our son. We found out what we already knew: no one, not even the "queen of autism," really had any answers for us.

I don't remember when it happened, but I started waking up at about 4:00 every morning. I would lie there and wonder what Matthew would be like at the age of ten or fifteen. I couldn't even imagine what he would be like or how our life with him would be when he was older. Would he still be in diapers? Would I still have to feed him, dress him and care for him for the rest of my life? Those thoughts were overwhelming at that point. How could I plan? How could I dream? It was almost more than I could bear. Gradually I learned that I could not think that far ahead. I had to take one day at a time. Each day truly brought new worries without me adding more of my own. My favorite Bible verse became Matthew 6:34 because it reads, "Therefore do not worry about tomorrow, for tomorrow will worry about itself. Each day has enough trouble of its own."

When Matt was two years old, he had acquired a limited vocabulary. Eventually we were able to record twenty-two words he had said at one time or another. Sometimes he would say a word once and then never say it again. He would say "ju" for juice at the babysitter's. He even put two words together "dada's tuck" for daddy's truck. One evening he came over and sat on my lap and said "Mom." That has been the one and only time I have ever heard him call me "Mom." When he was three and a half years old, Mel and I enrolled Matthew in some speech classes in Indianapolis. By this time he had lost the words he had said in the past. The people who worked there were wonderful. I stayed with Matthew and participated in activities with other children. Everything was hand over hand, and I walked him through different things the children did. No speech came, but it was another avenue that gave me a ray of hope for a while.

In the spring when Matt turned five years old, the teacher at Noble preschool starting talking about the next year. Matt would have to leave Noble and go to kindergarten somewhere else. His home school of Brownsburg did not offer any special education classes. The children with special needs either went to West Central Joint Services, whose populations was a conglomeration of students from our county and part of the next county, or they went to classes at Pike Township schools that were about thirty to forty minutes away. His teacher went with me to visit West Central Joint Services. It was a very old, dilapidated building on Washington Street on the west side of Indianapolis. We were given the big tour. The main thing I noticed was that many of the children were sorting squares from circles and gray objects from black objects. They weren't even colorful toys but drab pieces. I left with a feeling of determination. There was no way I wanted my precious son to go there to school. When I talked to the director a few days later, she insisted it would be the best placement for him. The only thing I really remember about the rest of the conversation was telling her that she was not going to make a factory worker out of my five year-old.

My husband and I were both very depressed and frustrated about Matt's future, and he was only five. We talked to the administrators at Noble. They suggested that we have a case conference with the Brownsburg School officials who were actually responsible for providing for his education since it was his home school. Two teachers from Noble, one being Matthew's current teacher, agreed to attend the conference with us. This is where life really began to get interesting. At that time I had been teaching elementary school at Brownsburg for about ten years. Now I had to go and deal with my own employer to do what was best for my son. Brownsburg at that time was a very conservative, small town. The male teacher who attended the conference with us had long hair and a beard – he looked like a hippie. Matthew's current teacher had a crazy, partly green hairdo. She wore lots of jewelry and the wildest painted fingernails. We definitely looked like a comical group as we entered the administration building at Brownsburg. The conference actually went fairly well, and during it, we decided that instead of going to West Central, Matt would go to an elementary school in Pike Township. Considering the other option at that point, we all were very pleased. He would be in a class for five-year-olds with special needs and would be mainstreamed occasionally into a regular kindergarten class. It really sounded pretty good.

CHAPTER 6

Dare We Try Again?

During Matt's time at Noble, we began thinking of having another child. Joey was a wonderful son and an excellent student. He truly seemed to be gifted. He was also a wonderful brother to Matt, delighting in each new step of progress his brother made. But I longed for another baby. My parents were very concerned about another pregnancy. They loved Matthew and Joey both so much, but they had also seen how Matthew's disability had affected our lives.

After talking to my OB/GYN, Mel and I made an appointment with a genetic counselor at Riley. He met with Matthew and us. He wanted to do some chromosomal studies before we tried to get pregnant. As it turned out, Matthew has part of an extra fifteenth chromosome, the p section. I accepted the verdict with mixed emotions. At first I was very depressed, because I knew that now there would be no hope for a "miracle cure." It wasn't just some developmental delays. It was a problem in every cell of his very being. But I also felt a wave of relief. This was not something I had done. It wasn't the wasp spray or the electric blanket or anything else. Whatever had gone wrong had happened at conception in the genetic makeup of the egg and sperm. I felt as if I was off the hook, so to speak, but at the same time, I felt that it was a life sentence for my child.

After getting our blood work done, the doctor said we were at no genetic risks of having another child with problems. So we went ahead and Katy was conceived in March of 2006. Again, I tried to do everything just right. I worried about everything. My father passed away from a heart attack early in my pregnancy. I know my friends and family worried about the impact that such a devastating emotional blow might have on my pregnancy. I started talking to my doctor about getting an amniocentesis done, knowing the cells could be checked for certain defects. My doctor strongly advised me not to go through with the procedure because it could have aborted the fetus. He told me that unless I would definitely consider aborting the fetus in case of abnormalities, I shouldn't do it. If I would not get an abortion, no matter the outcome, it would not be worth the risk.

After a lot of discussion and prayers, my husband and I decided to go ahead with it. Many days later, the genetic counselor's assistant called. She informed me that everything was fine. They had checked the fifteenth chromosomes in 10,000 of my baby's cells. What a relief! But the worry didn't stop there. While I was pregnant, I made many, many trips to Noble to pick up or take Matthew. I always saw children with all types of abnormalities there. The worries and the nightmares got worse as I neared the end of my pregnancy. I would dream that the baby was blind or physically deformed. One day I would want the baby to get here as soon as possible so I could stop worrying. Another day I wanted to postpone the birth as long as I could for fear of what might be. I had not wanted to know the sex of my baby. It did not matter one bit. I only prayed for a healthy baby this time, and I questioned how I would survive if it was not.

On December 18th I gave birth to a healthy little girl. I was thrilled. But after the joy and elation, the worrying set in once again. I looked for every sign that she was normal and any sign that she was not. Katy slept most of Christmas Day. It was hard to wake her up to nurse. By Christmas evening I was beside myself with worry. Why was she sleeping so much? The day after Christmas I called our doctor. He assured me she was a normal infant who just liked to sleep. The next major worry was that she was not holding her head up well enough. Every day I would put her on her stomach. Then I held up toys to see if she could pick her head up off of the table and support it. I took many pictures of her doing that just to reassure myself. Then one day I couldn't stand it any longer. I just knew she was not supporting her head as well as she could. In tears, I called Terry, my brother and the family physician. He said to bring her up to his house. I remember putting her belly first on my arm and flying her around gently like an airplane. The whole time her head was held up high, looking around at the room. My brother reassured me that she was doing great. Each new milestone that she conquered was a sigh of relief for me.

After all of my research about autism, however, I knew many autistic children started out normally, unlike Matthew, and then began to withdraw and lose speech. When Katy was three, talking in long sentences, doing everything ahead of schedule, I finally started to relax. The pregnancy had been difficult, but the months of watching her develop had been even harder. I was so happy to see her accomplishments but so scared they might begin to disappear. I thank God that we decided to have our little girl. It was a huge decision, filled with fear and worry, but also filled with hope for another happy, healthy child.

Not only has Katy been our pride and joy, but she has also had a huge impact on Matthew. We laugh now about how Katy learned to toddle around Matthew, frequently ducking her head. Matthew's favorite activity was to spin in circles holding a toy. Katy learned that she had to duck quickly or get clobbered. She still plays with him, loves him and encourages him. He responds to her in so many ways. For a brief time, Matthew would say Katy's name but then stopped. She has always brought out his smiles, his playfulness, and a side of Matthew that no one else can. To this day, Katy and Joey both have a very unique bond with their brother.

I love my brother and sister. They both encourage me to do my best. I am so lucky to have them. I hope when I get to heaven someday that I can spin Joey around on my shoulders and body slam him on the bed like he does to me. That would be fun. Even now when he body slams me, I feel like he loves me, because he treats me like an older brother should. Katy really watches out for me. She used to play with me every day even when I didn't want to. She forced me to really come out of my protective shell and do things with her. That was what I needed in order to become more social. Katy and Joey have both always found ways to show their love for me, and I am grateful to them.

CHAPTER 7

Failing to Recall – by Choice

I have just tried to forget the ages of five to eleven, because I was in special education classes in five different schools. It was the worst time of my life. Since I had no way to communicate, the teachers assumed I was retarded. I used to think I was, too. The other kids could talk, and they seemed different because they all had friends. Things were just different about me. I just did not belong with them. The fact that I couldn't talk was the most critical difference. The teachers tried to help me. All except one.

This teacher actually kept me strapped in a chair to keep me from spinning in circles. Spinning was so much fun for me. Spinning

still feels really good to me, even today. A lot of autistic people do things like this for a sense of relief from the stimulations that bombard us. The gravity, the noise and the lights can be overwhelming to our brains. Rocking or spinning relieves the anxiety. This teacher decided I should not do anything like that. She sat me in a chair with a tray in front of me. That was the worst thing I remember. I spent most of my day sitting confined to that chair. School had a very negative effect on me that year. I gave her discipline problems because this experience made my life seem hopeless. I acted awfully. I had no reason to try to behave. Finally, thanks to one of my former teachers, my parents heard what was happening to me at school. They talked to the principal, and then things changed. However, the year was almost over at that point.

When Matthew entered public school in Brownsburg, I thought that my being a teacher there might be an asset; since the other teachers and administrators knew me and I knew them, we might have an easier time working together. However, I soon found that I would be caught between a rock and a hard place many times. It was often difficult to disagree with the same school system that employed me. The first problem came almost immediately. Brownsburg would be transporting Matthew to Pike Schools. We were told that the bus driver would pick him up at 7:00 a.m., but school did not start until 9:00. According to the Director of Pupil Services, he would be picked up two hours before school started for a twenty-five minute trip to school. We were told, "If you can find a better way, do it." So my husband followed a special needs bus one morning and found that it arrived back at the bus barn by 8:30. He called the Director of Pupil Service and suggested that the bus stop for Matt at 8:30 after the regular route and run him to Pike instead of going back to the bus barn. They accepted the idea, but as was my nature, I worried that we had made the director mad. I did not like making enemies. I had no idea how many battles we would encounter within my own school system.

This is a perfect example of how parents should not simply accept what they are told. Mel and I have found over and over again that there are usually other solutions if people are willing to look for them. Most of the time, the only people who are willing to look are the parents. Therefore, parents just have to advocate for their special needs child.

Matt was in a class with a couple of other boys who had gone to Noble Preschool. I immediately recognized them and their mothers. As the year went on, the other two moms and I quickly bonded. We were not happy with the teacher at all. The only notes that came home were about how many accidents Matt had instead of using the potty. It was as if toileting was the main goal, if not the only goal, he was working toward that year. It was the next spring when she called us in for a conference. She had videotaped Matthew and all the things he could not do. She highly recommended that he be removed from her moderately mentally handicapped class and placed in a severe class at West Central, the very place we did not want our son to be. The impact of the video left us pretty much speechless. What else were we to do? She and her administrator were the professionals in this area. We did as we were told. At that point, I was not really sorry to see him leave Pike. I knew he would never progress as long as he was in that teacher's class.

Mel and I went to visit the classroom where Matthew would be placed at West Central. Mrs. Johnson, the teacher, seemed very kind and welcoming. I was immediately impressed with her and the activities going on in the classroom. Mrs. Johnson soon became my new light at the end of the tunnel. She noted progress, made constructive comments and encouraged us as parents. Instead of the negative daily notes that had come home, she often made positive remarks. I know she had to look hard to find positive things to say some days, but she managed to find them. I looked forward to reading about Matt's day at school. The year ended too soon for us even though he attended well into the summer. Mrs. Johnson was expecting a baby and would not be back the following year. That came as a crushing blow to us. In Matt's five to six years of life, we had already found out what a significant role his teachers would play not only in his progress, but our lives as well.

At the end of the summer, we were notified that Matt would go to a different school. They wanted the kids to be more integrated with normal children, so he would be attending Chapelwood Elementary School, a school in Wayne Township. He spent one year there, and then he and the class were uprooted and moved to Chapel Glen Elementary School. This would be his fourth different school. If there is anything he needed, it was structure. Changing schools every year or two was not providing him with that certainty in his life. However, the good news was that Mrs. Johnson was returning from her year of maternity leave, and Matt would be in her class again. That definitely made us feel better, but even though he was with an excellent teacher once again, we continued to see little progress from year to year.

The following year Matt was going to be in a new class with a different teacher. Mrs. Johnson was going to be moving to France with her husband for his new job later that year. Rather than leave in the middle of the school year, she had resigned. School began fairly well with few major conflicts between the teacher and me. I visited the class several times and went on a couple of field trips with them. It was hard to visit frequently because I was still teaching at Brownsburg at the same time.

One night in April I answered the phone, and to my surprise, it was Mrs. Johnson. She was leaving for France the next day. She had gone out to eat with a few teachers from Chapel Glen. She told me she couldn't leave for France until she called me first. The teachers had told her that Matt's current teacher kept him in a

Rifton chair, (a wooden chair with a seat belt and a tray in front), most of the day. He was strapped in it even at lunch. Mrs. Johnson knew how upset we would be and felt like we should know what was happening. Mel and I were devastated. We were angry that our son was going to school only to be strapped in a chair all day long. He had no way of telling us what was happening. We had blindly put our trust in the teacher and the school system.

The next morning Mel and I were waiting in the office when the principal arrived. We let her know that our son was fastened in a chair for most of the day. Of course she listened and tried to reassure us that there must have been a reason, but we knew that Matthew was not a danger to himself or others. He did not leave the room on his own. There was no reason for him to be strapped in a wooden chair. After a lengthy discussion, we were assured that this would not happen again. The rest of the school year was very long. We knew the teacher was upset with us, and we were very upset with how she had treated Matthew. The worst part was that we had had no idea what was happening in that room. Matthew went day after day to school and was strapped in a chair even for lunch and his nap, and he had no way to tell us. I am sure it was horrible for him. I cannot imagine anything much more frustrating than being locked in silence.

CHAPTER 8

Hope

In the midst of that ordeal, my mother happened to read an article in the Indianapolis newspaper about a boy who went to school in Warren Township. He was very similar to Matt. He was autistic and spoke only a small amount of words. He had a special education teacher, Laura Poorman, who had been trained in a method called facilitated communication at Syracuse University in New York. With her hand supporting this boy's hand, he was able to type words and sentences out on the computer. No one, not even his parents, had known he was capable of spelling and reading. I read the article in amazement. I knew that there was no way Matthew could spell words or even know the alphabet. He had never seemed to have any interest in listening to me read stories, as I had always done with my other children. He would never sit still beside me and pay attention. Consequently, I assumed he wasn't interested. Mel and I read the article, and I started to throw it away. However, I changed my mind and put it under one of my cabinets in the kitchen where I kept some of the important papers.

One day near the end of May, I came across the article. I read it again and thought, "What do I have to lose?" I decided to call the teacher at Warren Township as soon as I got a chance. School was ending so things were very busy. The last day of school, when the children were gone, leaving the teachers to work on records, I went down to the office to use the phone. I talked to the receptionist at the school where Laura Poorman worked. I left a message and waited. That evening I got the call I had been waiting for. We discussed Matthew at length. I told her about his diagnosis of "severely mentally handicapped" and about how he did not talk or even point to things; that basically he had no way to communicate with us. The more I talked, the more she said Matthew sounded a lot like her student Seth. We agreed to meet at the end of June. She was leaving on a vacation so it would be a few weeks until she returned. A part of me was so hopeful, but the realist part of me thought that there was no way that Matthew would be able to type words.

It was a long few weeks. Finally she called me, and we scheduled a meeting on June 29, 1993 at 1:00. We were going to meet at her student's house so we could watch him type. Then Laura asked me if I had told Matthew about meeting with her. Of course, I hadn't – why would I? The thought never really crossed my mind. As soon as I hung up the phone, I went and talked to Matt about our scheduled meeting. He showed no response, which was pretty much par for the course.

I was hopeful when I heard that I might have a chance to communicate. One day my mom told me she was going to take me to see a discovery called facilitated communication. The word "communication" actually excited me even though I did not understand what facilitated meant. There was a teacher named Laura Poorman in Warren Township in Indianapolis, Indiana who was using facilitated communication with a student. She was going to show me a way to possibly communicate. My mom said that we were going to meet with this teacher and that she wanted to try this system of communication with me. What a glorious moment that was! I was so excited. All I knew was that I couldn't wait to try it.

First of all, I have autism and am nonverbal. As I said, as a child I could not even point to things or pictures. When I was in preschool, teachers wanted me to point to a body part. For example, they would ask me to point to my ear. I knew exactly where it was, but my brain could not find a way to allow me to move my

hand to it. This became difficult, as did other requests. Even today I have trouble following commands that are not part of my routine. The problem is not the understanding. The sensory nerves work fine. A connection is not made between my brain and muscles.

The day arrived and we drove to the other side of Indianapolis. I pulled up in front of the house. I was so nervous and apprehensive, not knowing what to expect. My biggest concern was whether Matt would be alright bathroom-wise. I never made a trip anywhere without worrying about an occasional accident.

Seth's mother welcomed us into her home. We met Seth, his brother and sister and Laura Poorman. We talked for a few minutes introducing ourselves. Then Poorman, as Matthew grew to call her, sat down with Seth at his computer. She sat on his right and supported his hand by slipping her hand into his palm. She pushed Seth's hand back to his shoulder. She asked him a question, and he began to push his hand and hers down to the keyboard. Later she moved her hand back and just gently touched his elbow. Seth typed, talking directly to Matt and me.

As I watched, the pessimism or skepticism in me immediately came out. I knew it had to be some hocus-pocus. This boy spoke some but only in one or two word phrases, most having nothing to do with what he was typing. Then Laura had Matthew sit down beside her. She talked to him about how she thought he was probably a very bright boy but had trouble communicating. She explained how she hoped this new method of facilitated communication would help him to express himself. Matt never used his index finger to point. So she curled his other three fingers up in his palm and placed her hand over them to keep them in place, isolating his index finger. She brought his hand back to his shoulder and asked him to spell his name. With her pushing his hand back to his shoulder and offering resistance, he had to really push to be able to touch a key on the keyboard. One letter at a time, with his hand brought back to his shoulder after each letter, he typed M A T T H E W. I couldn't believe it. I just sat and stared as he answered a few more questions with her. I just could not bring myself to believe he was the one doing the typing.

I began using facilitated communication (FC) on June 29, 1993. At eleven years old I was able to speak, by typing, for the first time. First I watched a boy type with Poorman facilitating. A sudden attack of hope filled my heart. Then the teacher sat down with me. I felt the pressure against my hand, and performing FC for the first time, I typed my name the best I could. We typed for a long time, and I kept getting better and better at it. Poorman showed my mom how to hold my hand. The teacher had me tell my mom something that I had always

wanted to tell her – I finally got to tell my mom that I loved her.

After about thirty minutes, Poorman asked me to try facilitating with Matt. She instructed me how to sit and hold his hand as she had done, isolating the index finger. I asked him to tell me something. He typed, "I love you." I could feel his hand pushing mine toward each key as I brought his hand back to his shoulder and offered resistance. He was pushing my hand toward each letter. There was no doubt that he was doing the typing.

What totally amazed me was that Matthew sat at that computer forty-five minutes with us. This was a boy who could not focus his attention on anything more than a few minutes, if that. Poorman asked him why he liked to hold pictures in frames up to his nose and walk around with them the way he did. He had been doing that while we took a break. He said he liked to see the reflections. Sure enough, we tried it ourselves and you could see all different parts of the room reflected in the glass. She asked him if he liked cake and ice cream. He said, "No." She looked at me. Sure enough, he did not like either. His answers to questions like that started making me believe that maybe it really was Matthew doing the typing.

I could hardly wait to get home and tell Mel, Joey and Katy. I called my mother immediately as well. I was hesitant to share the news with my friends or anyone else though. It almost seemed too good to be true.

A part of me still could not believe it was Matthew typing. He had never visibly shown any interest in letters or in reading. Then I got to thinking about other signs that he was learning on his own. His favorite book was a fifth grade math book I had brought home from school one time. It was blue. He loved fingering through the pages. We had gone through several of those books in the last couple of years. If we closed the book, he could go right back and find the page he had been looking at. He also loved looking at a dictionary we had. He would spend a lot of time just flipping through the pages. His favorite show on TV was *Wheel of Fortune*. He also would stop whatever he was doing and listen to stories being reported on the news. He loved listening to the weather report. At the babysitter's he always watched *Sesame Street* and the *Electric Company* with the other children. We had no idea that any of that information was sinking into his brain.

On June 29, 1993 Matt had a new birthday. He was truly entering our world for the first time.

CHAPTER 9

Fact or Fantasy

Getting my first chance to speak was a moment that gave me hope that my life would change. A whole new world was there, waiting for me. I no longer had to live my life in silence. The happiness I felt was giving me new life. My mother and I worked all summer on facilitated communication. The hardest thing, though, was having so much to say and still not always being able to say it all. Facilitating is not easy and takes much time and practice.

Facilitated communication saved my life, and I know it has saved some others' lives. Some people who are unable to communicate in any

other way use this method. However, it is still very controversial. Most people think this method of communication is totally invalid, but for some people, and with trained facilitators, it can work very well. The theory that FC is definitely invalid can destroy the hopes that many autistic people have to communicate with the world around them.

Facilitated communication actually means that a facilitator supports the communicator's hand or arm so that the individual can press the keys on a computer keyboard or some other type of device, such as a letter board or typewriter. Facilitators provide physical support at the wrist, hand, arm or elbow. Support comes in the form of pressure. The facilitator pushes the hand or arm back toward the shoulder. Resistance actually "supports" as this causes the disabled individual to force the movement to the correct keys. It enables the person to point more effectively. FC requires the touch of another person. Eventually this support can be faded to just a light touch.

Facilitated communication was designed for people who have little or no speech. Some autistic studies have shown that intelligence is hidden because of a lack in communication skills. Rosemary Crossley started using facilitated communication with nonverbal people in Australia. Syracuse University started trying

this method in the United States in 1989. When Douglas Biklen, Director of Special Education at Syracuse, learned about this method, he started using it with autistic students near the university. As it gained success, facilitated communication spread into the rest of the United States, Canada and Europe.

Facilitated communication really has opened a door for many communication-impaired individuals. People living with autism, cerebral palsy and Down's Syndrome have had an opportunity to show others how much they really do know. FC has given people the chance to open their secret inner selves, and that has given their lives meaning. Being able to communicate for the nonverbal is like seeing for the blind or hearing music for the deaf.

Having no way to communicate is like being trapped under a concrete slab; silence is torture for those who can think but can't speak. Not speaking usually means that a person is dumb and mute. FC put an end to that. Individuals who were thought to be retarded have been found to have intelligence no one suspected. It seems too good to be true. Sometimes when people cannot explain something, they become doubtful; researchers could not explain how FC worked, so their doubts and skepticism grew. Opponents began criticizing and questioning the method. Why would someone

who acted mentally handicapped suddenly be able to know all of this information? Are facilitators subconsciously or consciously moving the hand of the person typing? Can FC really work? Many people will not accept FC as true communication.

Before I learned to use facilitated communication, I had thought that special education was going to be my future, and that seemed like the worst fate in the world to me. Even my own family did not know I was "in there." I had often wondered if the door was always going to be shut because there was no way to let people actually understand what I knew.

Every day after we first met with Poorman, I typed with Matt. I started asking him questions like, "Do you know how old you are?" I showed him pictures and asked him to name them: toothbrush, elephant, football. He could name everything I showed him. I wrote the words for furniture and appliances in the house with the correct spelling for him to see. He didn't need any of that. He knew it already. I kept a journal of all of my questions and all of his answers. I did not want to forget a single thing that he typed. I honestly felt like I was in an episode of the *Twilight Zone*. Some nights I was almost afraid to go to sleep; I was afraid to wake up and find it had just been a dream.

Each day brought out more information that Matthew knew. It just didn't seem possible that he had been able to absorb so much knowledge on his own. We met with Poorman every two weeks. I longed for those meetings so much. I couldn't wait to tell her things that Matthew had typed, and I loved watching her type with him. One time she had typed a letter to Matthew. It was on the computer monitor when we arrived. She and I talked and Matthew stood and occasionally glanced at the screen. When he sat down with her to type, he started responding to what she had written. He could read sentences! I was so excited. It made sense that if he knew how to spell words, he might also know how to read, but at that point, it was beyond my wildest imagination. Matthew never really looked at books in the usual way. Most people read one page at a time and turn the page, but Matthew flipped back and forth in the book or had it turned sideways when he looked at it.

I started reading books to Matthew – not picture books, but works of literature including *To Kill a Mockingbird* and *All Quiet on the Western Front*. He loved being read to. He would sit up on the bed beside me or on the floor next to the sofa and rock back and forth. If I quit reading, he would pick up the book and hand it to me again. It was like now that he knew that I knew that he was in there, it brought out a whole new sense of excitement and a thirst for more knowledge.

He once typed, "I know there is hope for me now. I'm so glad you found me in here." Now when I reflect back on Matt's statement, it makes me feel so grateful that we were introduced to facilitated communication. It led us to finding our son. He was there all along but might never have been found. I often wonder how many other people with autism lived and died without ever being discovered. It makes me sick thinking about those who never had a chance to let people know that they, too, were in there. I'm sure there are now many other people with autism who have so much knowledge, if only they were given the opportunity to reveal it. I am sure that the skepticism surrounding facilitated communication has prevented many teachers and families from pursuing its use with their students or children. I am so thankful that I finally took that article out of my cabinet and made the phone call to Laura Poorman.

That summer was the most exciting summer of my life. As I told friends and family about out discovery, almost everyone reacted the same way, with goose bumps. At times I just still could not believe it was possible for this boy, diagnosed as severely mentally handicapped, to now have all of this knowledge about the world around him. All along, it had been there, but he had had no way to let us know.

Joey and Katy had fun asking him all kinds of questions to see what he knew. Joey loved to ask him questions about sports, such as, "How many world championships has Michael Jordan won?" Matthew knew the answer. He also knew about Desert Storm and the war in Kuwait. We found computer games that Joey and Katy could play with Matt as I facilitated for him. One of their favorites was *Family Feud*. They loved seeing the answers that Matthew would come up with during the game.

After quizzing him constantly and trying to pick his brain, I finally asked him if there was something he wanted to ask me. He typed, "Will I ever get to be a daddy?" I just sat there with a huge lump rising in my throat. When I gave him the opportunity to ask me something, I had no idea what to expect. That heart-wrenching question was certainly the farthest thing from my mind. Here was my son, eleven years old, locked within himself until now, and that was his first question. I had no idea how to respond. At that point I truly did not know what was possible in the future, and that's what I told him. I no longer knew what his capabilities would someday be. We would just take things one day at a time and see where we were headed.

CHAPTER 10

Normal School for a Not-so-Normal Kid

Finally after about six weeks of typing with Matt and working with Poorman, I knew I had to call the assistant superintendent of Brownsburg schools. She was well aware of my son and his disability. When I called her, I asked her if she had time to talk with me because I had something important to share with her. She listened to my story unfold for almost an hour. Of course, she agreed with me that Matthew would need more than a special education class when school started. She said she would set the wheels in motion. I was ecstatic with her response and enthusiasm.

Before school officially started, Mel, Matt, and I met with the principal, assistant principal, and a third grade teacher I had long respected, Pat Kilian. Matt was going to be placed in her class. Even though Matt was eleven, we agreed that third grade would be a good starting place for him, based on what we knew so far about his abilities. It couldn't have been a better placement.

Before the new school year began, my parents and I attended a case conference at Eagle Elementary. I got to participate using FC. A woman who had once questioned FC even asked me how to spell a word for her. I felt pretty good knowing how to spell a word that she didn't know. The case conference committee decided that the best placement for me would be in third grade since they really did not know what level of skills I had. "Wonderful" was the word I chose to describe my feelings at that moment. The rest of the conference was a blur for me, as all of my attention was focused on absorbing the reality of this dream come true.

Before school started, the director of student services wanted Matt to take an intelligence test. In the past he had scored extremely low because he had had no way to communicate his answers. We still wondered whether this time would be different. We were sent to Children's Resource Group in Indianapolis, and I had no idea whether or not the people there would allow me to facilitate with Matt. If it was like the previous type of testing, nothing would be different. The results would still show that he was severely mentally handicapped. When we met the director of the resource group, I immediately liked her. She asked many good questions and seemed genuinely excited about our new discovery with Matt. She was not going to do the testing though; another woman in her office would. They decided that I could facilitate with Matt on most of the tests.

To begin, the woman tried to get Matt to manipulate blocks and puzzle pieces. I had to remain in the waiting room. She quickly found out that Matthew could not do any of that, so we began the next tests. They administered several tests, including the Peabody Picture Vocabulary test and the Wechsler Intelligence Scale. Sometimes Matt had to choose one of four pictures that best described a given word. Matt would respond by typing the names of the number corresponding to his answer. At times he would interject comments such as he was scared or wanted to stop. She asked Matt many questions about the world around us, such as, "In which direction does the sun rise?" Later he had to identify pictures and sequences. She had a folder up in front of her scoring pad for the test. Sometimes when Matt did not know an answer, he would type, "I don't know," and eventually he started typing "IDK" when he did not know. All of a sudden she started laughing and said, "I need to cover up my notes better." I could not see her papers, but Matthew had seen that when he said, "I don't know," she would jot down "IDK" on her pad. I had not seen it, but obviously Matt had and started using that response. That definitely helped convince her that it was Matt, not his mother, doing the typing. Matt was asked if he knew what caused rust. He typed another answer I will never forget. He responded, "The same thing that we breathe." She asked what that was and he replied, "Oxygen." She was definitely impressed, and so was I. After one of the more complicated questions, Matthew answered it and then responded, "Some question." We had to meet with her three times to complete the test due to the slowness of his typing. Also, he was not used to sitting very still for long periods of time.

After the testing was completed, the director of Children's Resource Group and the school administrators met with us. The final report showed that Matt was average or slightly above average in intelligence. This was a long way from his diagnosis of "severely mentally retarded." After some of his responses were shared with the people at the conference, I think everyone walked away with a new respect for what Matthew could do academically.

It was the fifth school I had been to. I was in the special education class at the beginning of each day, and then I went to my third grade class. My special education teacher was new to the school, as was the program. She was an older woman who seemed to be very firm and strict. She usually spoke in a gruff voice, and the first time I met her I was scared, but she

ended up being the best teacher I had in special education.

Laura Poorman started working with the aides in that class. She showed the three of them how to facilitate. One of them was especially good at it. Her name was Laura Scott. Laura Scott was my first facilitator at Brownsburg. She was so funny. We used to "talk" and make jokes. She learned quickly how to support my hand so I could communicate what I wanted to.

Students in my third grade class did not really understand who I was or why I was there. Even though I have above average intelligence, I don't really seem normal. The worst thing is a problem I have with low muscle tone that makes me drool sometimes. The kids did not understand why I did that.

What I worried about most was acting correctly. I had never been in a classroom with regular kids, so I had no idea what to expect or how to act. At first they were shy around me. Fortunately that changed. They soon found out that I was smart, and they accepted me. The teacher, Mrs. Kilian, also accepted me. She scared me at first; I was trying so hard to do what I was supposed to do. The teacher and students eventually treated me as if I was a normal kid. Was I ever excited! Going to a regular class was the miracle that I had always hoped for. It was like everything came alive. The happiest

time of my life was when the children asked me questions, and I got to actually carry on a conversation. The best part of this whole new life was getting to learn the same as the "normal" kids.

I only spent a couple of hours each day in that class for reading and spelling. We always talked a while before starting the spelling work. I knew how to spell a lot of the words, and I knew what a lot of them meant too. I so loved to read the dictionary, and a lot of times I remembered the meanings. Usually when Mrs. Kilian called on me, I would give definitions for the spelling words that I had read in the dictionary. When I gave answers, I would type on a letter board. This is a piece of construction paper with squares on it. There is a letter in each square, and when I wanted to say something, I would point to the letters using FC.

When I was first starting FC, I met with Laura Poorman frequently. One time she let me use a Canon Communicator. It really was awesome. The Canon had a small keyboard and a tape that printed what I typed. It was small so that you could carry it with you. One day I typed to my class that I wanted one. I told them it was called a Canon Communicator. My class decided they wanted to raise money to buy one for me. It would cost about $1,000.

The other students wanted a chance to earn money to buy it for me, so Mrs. Kilian asked my mom if it would be alright with her and my dad. They agreed. The kids earned money by reading books for a monetary amount from a set pledge. Some of them wanted to write letters and send them to the newspaper. Because of the letters, people started contributing money. Each day more and more money came to the school. My classmates also had a garage sale at school to get more donations. By doing all of these projects, the kids earned a little over $2,000. They decided to buy me two communicators, one for school and one for home. They called their campaign "From the Heart." The class wanted to give them to me on Valentine's Day, so on February 14, 1994, the kids and I went to the cafeteria. It was decorated with balloons. My mom and dad were invited. A few other parents came and brought cookies and punch. My class sat with me on the steps to the stage. This was such a wonderful day for me. While we sat on the steps to the stage, and Mrs. Kilian made the presentation, I was overcome with happiness. The Canons were such great gifts, but the greatest gift was their friendship. It truly did come from the heart. I have always treasured the memories of that wonderful day.

After I got the Canons, I used them to communicate and do my homework. The kids always wanted to see what I had said, and they wanted the strip of paper showing the words I typed. A few weeks later we heard that Channel 6 was going to send a reporter to the school to do a story on what the class had done for me. The mother of a girl in my class had called them and told them about the story.

I was so scared. The story could be good for facilitated communication, but what worried me was that the story might do more harm than good. In the fall 60 Minutes had done a show about facilitated communication. I had been afraid to watch it, but my parents wanted me to. The show made FC look like a hoax. The man, who was interviewed, worked with disabled people who had communication disorders. He had a PhD from Syracuse University, the same university where Doug Biklen worked. This man set out to prove that facilitated communication was not valid. He conducted experiments where a disabled person was shown a picture. Then this person, by typing, had to tell the facilitator, who had not seen the picture, what the picture was. He showed that the facilitator and the disabled person almost consistently failed this "blind test." Therefore, he concluded the method was not a scientifically valid technique.

As I watched the show, I was furious and disheartened, because I knew there was evi-

dence that did exist to prove that facilitated communication does work for some people. I have typed things that my facilitator has not known. This is not formal testing but can and has validated that I do the typing. Also, some individuals who were facilitating can now type independently. Other individuals can type with a facilitator's hand on their shoulder. (I can't do that yet but hope to some day.) There is not a scientific explanation as to why that hand is necessary, but it works for some people. Other strange things happen without scientifically demonstrated support. For example, an individual with autism who I know has the gift of playing the organ extremely well. There is no scientific explanation as to how he can play so well, but he can do it.

Because of the negative controversy, communication has been taken away from many nonverbal, disabled people. Some autistic people tragically lost their desperately needed ability to communicate. Communicating is the key so many of us are searching for. Giving us a hope and then stripping us of that hope is cruel.

When the students in the class saw the program, they were very angry. Mrs. Kilian had the students write letters explaining the reasons that people should believe that FC works. The program never responded to their letters.

As much as I wanted Channel 6 to show that FC does really work for some people, I hoped the reporter would interview just the kids and not me. I was nervous and scared. I was afraid she might not think it was me doing the typing. A reporter came to the school with a cameraman. She talked to Mrs. Kilian and the kids about autism and the campaign to raise the money. She also interviewed my mother. My mother told her about the time I had typed, "I'm so glad you found me in here." She also asked the reporter to please give FC a chance so as to not discourage others from trying it. Then the reporter even tried typing with me. When she finished, she said she could feel me push her hand to the letters.

That afternoon the story appeared on the news, and it was great. I was so surprised and relieved.

That year in third grade was the best year ever. The children in that classroom took Matthew under their caring wings, thanks to the guidance of a wonderful teacher. Mrs. Kilian was just what Matthew needed to get his regular education program off to a great start. Not only did she accept Matthew and work with his autism, but she also encouraged the children and staff to support Matthew. The "From the Heart" campaign touched so many people, but especially our family.

Mrs. Kilian was the first of many wonderful, special people we have met as a result of Matthew's disability. That is one thing I feel very thankful for – all of those people we have met along the way and never would have known if not for Matthew's handicap. There have been so many men and women who I feel God has placed in our lives to help us. I would like to think that Matthew has helped others discover some of their unknown talents. I think that knowing him and working with him has made them realize what a gift they have to offer others.

The administrators at Eagle Elementary School were also very instrumental in Matthew's success. When Matthew would act up in class or was just having what we came to call an "autistic day," he would go down to the office and sit in a room. Mrs. Rickman and Mrs. Sanders had read that turning off the fluorescent lights can help a child calm down. So they would let him sit with the lights off. They often laughed and told me how they would step out of the room to talk about Matt. They always thought it was remarkable how he instantly quieted down in order to hear what they were saying.

Dear Friends,

We have a friend whose name is Matt. He wants a Canon Communicator. He is an autistic child. He is a great speller. We are trying to earn money for him. We are calling this "From The Heart". We realey would hope you could help us. We would like to give it to him by Valentine's Day. This Canon Communicator prints out what he says.

Your friend,

Dear Friends,

We are trying to earn enough to buy a Canon Communicator. A Canon Communicator is a thing to help autistic people. We have a friend named Matt, and we want to buy it for him. He goes to Eagle Elementary. He is very smart, but he can't talk. If you know a way to help us, that would be great. We want to earn enough money by Valentine's Day. I'm in Mrs. Kilian's class. We're going to have a garage sale to raise money

Your friend,

Dear Friends,

Hello! I'm I'm in Mrs. Kilian's third grade class at Eagle Elementary School. We have a boy named Matt in our class. He is autistic. He is smart and intelligent, but he can not speak. He uses a letter board. Matt has told us about a thing called a Canon Communicator. It is similar to a computer. The reason Matt wants this is because it types on the screen what he is saying. The Canon is 900 dollars. We are going to try and get that much money by having a garage sale and other stuff. We are hop you will give donations to us. It wo help if you did. Thank you.

Sincerely,

CHAPTER 11

My Friend Todd

My year in third grade was awesome. Mrs. Kilian was as responsible as anyone for my success. She always believed in FC and gave me a chance to show that I belonged in a regular class. She showed such kindness and understanding. She demonstrated the respect and compassion that served as a model for the kids in my class. Many of them gave me not only their respect but also their friendship. The greatest thing of all was the friendship that developed in that third grade class with Todd Lentz.

I forget how the friendship began. Todd was in my third grade class. I liked him, and he

seemed to like me. Todd took an interest in developing a friendship outside of school. He and his mother asked my mom if we would go to Pizza King with them. He enjoyed autistic me and liked talking to me as my mom facilitated our discussion, and that made me unbelievably happy. He was the first real friend I ever had.

I believe that having Mrs. Kilian as my third grade teacher was the best thing that could have happened to me. She believed in my typing and did so much to encourage me. I found myself surrounded by a love I had not known existed. The kids in my class found that doing good deeds for someone else was rewarding, and we all got so much out of that year. I know that they will never understand fully what their love meant to me.

Matthew opened people's eyes all along his educational path. At Eagle Elementary I think there were some staff members who questioned Matthew's abilities. He looked and acted mentally handicapped. It had taken me, his own mother, months to convince myself that he really had average or above intelligence. No one had ever really seen anyone like Matthew. The mindset is that if you look and act retarded, you probably are retarded. I don't blame anyone for feeling that way; that's the way I had always felt too.

One day at school Matthew typed, with his aide Laura Scott, that he thought he had strep throat. Laura wrote home to tell me what he had typed. I felt his forehead, and he was cool. He ate dinner just fine. The next day he typed the same thing several times. Again when he came home, he felt cool and seemed alright. The next day was the same. I called my brother Terry, who is a doctor, to see if he would look at Matthew's throat. I told him that it was crazy, but he kept typing at school that his throat hurt, so Terry looked down his throat. This is no easy task. Matt will let a nurse draw blood and barely flinch, but he refuses to open his mouth to let anyone look down his throat. While I held his arms, Terry pried his mouth open with a tongue depressor. Sure enough, his throat was red with white pussy spots. He was immediately put on antibiotics. Evidently this story spread throughout Eagle and made a believer of many a Doubting Thomas.

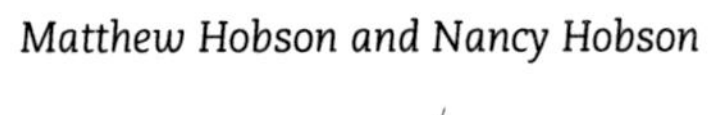

CHAPTER 12

Three Little Words

Matthew would often speak parts of sentences randomly. He would say, "And I have..." and then the rest of the sentence was gibberish. He loved to talk loudly in the bathtub. I think he liked the sound of his voice in the enclosed area. We would often hear words that we recognized. When Matt would speak his gibberish, he would use expression and intonation. It was just like he was carrying on a conversation, but we could not understand any of it. He had the whole idea of communication, but it usually didn't come out in any recognizable form.

When Matt started facilitating, he would say the names of some of the letters out loud. I would hear e, t, a and a few others. He had never done that before. It was so validating to me that he knew exactly what he was spelling and typing.

Many mornings he would get up early and walk into our bedroom. He would be saying a part of a sentence such as, "And we went..." A few months after he began facilitating, the most wonderful thing happened. My husband and I were trying to sleep in, something that rarely happened with our early-rising son, and Matt came into the bedroom. He came around to my side of the bed, and I lay there, pretending to still be asleep. All of a sudden he took his index finger, his typing finger, and touched me on the shoulder. With each touch, he verbally said a letter aloud. He typed on my shoulder and said the letters, "I-L-O-V-E-... U"

Three little words. I love you. Most of us have heard them often, whether they're spoken on television, or by a spouse, parent or child. Sometimes they are spoken very lovingly with endearment, and other times they are spoken quickly out of habit without much thought or feeling, at the end of a phone call perhaps. These three small words I had heard so often from others, but they never sounded as sweet as they did that morning. During that one special moment in time, those words were far from ordinary.

Another exciting event occurred during Matthew's year in third grade. He started greeting people verbally. He would say, "Hi! How are you?" This happened for a few months, and then just as suddenly as it had appeared, it disappeared. We have never heard it again. It was like for a brief instant someone had flipped on the switch in his brain, and there were understandable words. Then, just as quickly, the switch was turned off. The best thing was that we knew he had the potential for speech. He could do it at times. However, it was also very frustrating. We knew he could do it, but we had no idea how to help him. To this day, we still don't. It's also been discouraging because as he's gotten older he has lost all of the words and phrases he used to vocalize. The last word we have heard is "hot." He would say that when he stuck his foot into the bath water sometimes. Even that word has now disappeared from usage.

Many of the same kids from my third grade class were in my fourth grade class, and that was great. They made me feel less nervous. I had a new teacher and a new facilitator, both of whom I liked. I was selected to be in the Spell Bowl that year. I was given a long list of words to learn. I knew most of them, probably by reading the dictionary. The contest was at the school I attended. All the fourth grade classes in the school corporation were competing. Each class had chosen students to represent them. I was feeling very nervous at the contest that day. The students from other buildings at the contest had never seen me type with facilitated communication. I was worried that they might not think, as many don't, that I was the one doing the typing. When the time came for

me to spell my six words, the idea came to me to miss some of the words so they might believe it was actually my typing. I even missed the word "spaghetti", which was ridiculous because spaghetti was my favorite food, and I typed it frequently. I did the word without the "h" because that is the mistake my teacher said most kids make. This contest was so fun for me because it was a chance for me to be in front of many people and show them how I facilitated what I wanted to say. It also introduced many other people to facilitated communication.

When Matthew was in fourth grade, there was a facilitated communication conference that was going to be held at Syracuse University in New York. I mentioned it to the assistant principal, Mrs. Sanders. The next thing I knew I was making arrangements for both her and me to go to the conference. We flew to Syracuse and attended a three-day conference. It was an amazing time. We met people from all over the world who used facilitated communication to help them or their children communicate. A few of the people we met were now typing with just a touch on the elbow or shoulder. It was so exciting to hear how the method of communication originated and the effects it had had on so many people. Mrs. Sanders and I both left feeling enlightened and very happy that we had attended. All that we learned served to reinforce what Matthew was doing and that facilitated communication could help others like him.

When my mom and Mrs. Sanders went to Syracuse University to an FC conference, they decided I should skip fifth grade the next year and go to sixth grade. Finally I was going to be more challenged. I was put in Mrs. Barbarich's class at her request. The nicest teacher in sixth grade wanted me in her class! You can't imagine how thrilling that idea was to me. That was definitely an ego booster. By skipping a grade, the kids would be new to me, and I would be new to them.

That would prove to be the second best school year, but I was sad because school at Eagle Elementary would soon be over. We took an interesting field trip that year to a courthouse to hear real court cases with juveniles who had committed crimes. The best part was seeing a real judge. When we began talking about the trip, the kids were so excited, but I was concerned about going and having to sit still that long. Mrs. Barbarich wanted me to get to go, and she thought I could do it. I was so glad that she really trusted me. I tried to do my best for her, and the trip was a success.

The school also had a camping program for sixth graders at Bradford Woods during the week of Halloween. The kids would spend three days and two nights there. Everybody had anticipated this trip during the years of school

prior to sixth grade. I really wanted to go with my class.

We were going to be gone during Halloween. My friend Todd, who was now in fifth grade, had said he wanted to take me trick-or-treating. I thought that was the nicest thing he could have done. There was only one problem. I wanted to go to camp too. So my parents decided I could go to camp one day and night and then go home for Halloween.

The kids included me in everything at camp. They were thrilled when the lady in charge of our group asked who had dogs for pets. I raised my hand at the appropriate time, something I had never done. The other kids thought that that was great. They were always so happy to see signs of my progress. I really had fun on that trip.

At the end of Matt's fourth grade year, the principal told me that a sixth grade teacher actually had requested to have Matthew in her classroom. Just that statement made me feel so happy and encouraged about the year ahead. Matthew would be with a different group of students, but they would prove to be equally accepting. In sixth grade the students went to Bradford Woods to camp for three days and two nights. I wanted Matt to have the experience, so I took time off from my job and went with Matthew the first day. The leaders at the camp engaged the students in a lot of activities that required them to work together as a group. I loved watching how they included Matt. One activity involved the use of an inner tube taken from inside a tire. The group joined hands and could not let go as they passed the inner tube from one of their bodies to the next. It was quite challenging for any child, let alone Matthew. But the group came together, encouraged him and got the job done. He was so happy to be part of the group. At one point, our group leader asked who had a dog. Matthew, who had never raised his hand at the appropriate time, actually lifted his hand into the air. The kids exclaimed, "Look! Matthew raised his hand, and he has a dog!" They were as excited as I was to see him do this. Later that night we sat around a campfire. Matthew laid his head down on another student's lap. It didn't seem to bother her at all. She just rubbed his back as he rested there. Mel came down then and spent the night in the boys' cabin. It was such a wonderful experience for Matthew and for us as well. It was so wonderful to see the other students include Matt.

Matt left camp the next afternoon because it was Halloween, and his best friend from his third and fourth grade class had wanted to go trick-or-treating with him. Can you imagine a ten year-old boy wanting to go trick-or-treating with someone who could not talk to him and actually interacted very little? This was the way Todd Lentz was. He had befriended Matthew early in third grade. He and his mother would pick up Matthew and me, and we would go out for pizza on the weekends or during the summer. He was such a kind and loving boy. He also facilitated some with Matt so that they could communicate with each other. So Matt insisted on leaving camp on Halloween afternoon so that he could go trick-or-treating around the neighborhood with his friend.

Todd was another one of those very special people we probably would have never known if we had not had Matt. He continued to be friends with him through junior high.

CHAPTER 13

On to Junior High

I was sad as the year concluded because there had been so many happy memories for me in elementary school. I had grown so much during those three years, and for the first time in my life, I had gotten to do so many things that the other students had always been able to do. I will never forget the staff for accepting me as I was and for treating me the way they treated the other kids. They facilitated my development, and I went from being considered "retarded" to being considered a normal student.

In the spring of my last year there, the assistant principal began trying to find a new

facilitator for me. The current facilitator was not going to go to the junior high. She had been with me for two years. I hated the idea of having to break in a new one. Realizing the importance of the job, Mrs. Sanders immediately started searching for a replacement, and that was a good thing, because the job is not an easy one. The most important requirement was believing that an autistic, nonverbal boy could actually do the work of a sixth grader. The first woman to try facilitating didn't really believe that someone as autistic as I was could actually have the ability to do sixth grade work. She did the typing herself with her finger while holding my hand. That was indescribably frustrating. A conscientious assistant saw her and told the assistant principal who did not ask this woman to return.

Soon she called another woman named Brenda. I liked her immediately. She was so good at facilitating with me – she was the best person I had had so far which was comforting since I would be starting in a new building. The hardest part of moving to a new building was proving myself again.

At the end of sixth grade, Matt had to get a new facilitator. The principal started interviewing people for the position. Again, the school system was so helpful in wanting to make sure that Matt's success continued in junior high. They found a woman who was interested in trying to facilitate with Matt for a few days to see if she would like the job. I could tell from what Matt was typing at home that he was not impressed with her at all. Facilitating is not an easy skill to learn, and there are some people who are just not cut out for it.

Next they found a woman who had been a stay-at-home mom and was now ready to get a job in the school system. Brenda was very attractive, and Matthew took an instant liking to her. Laura Poorman came up that summer and trained Brenda in facilitating. She and Matthew got along very well.

CHAPTER 14

My Special Education Teacher

I was fortunate to have such a good facilitator in junior high. Brenda did so well facilitating with me, and she was fun to be with. The first time Brenda and I went to class, we were both so scared and worried because I was taking a pre-algebra class, but Brenda did a great job helping me figure out how to do the math on the keyboard of the computer.

I have always enjoyed doing math. There is something really intriguing to me about numbers. The concreteness of them gives me a belief in the order of the world. I feel like solving equations helps me to sort through things

that are usually complicated for me. The math equations tend to make more sense than the rest of the world does. When I was very young, I loved flipping through the pages of a fifth grade math book. I got so I could solve the equations and problems in my head. I found math to be very soothing.

I missed the students I had been with in my class at Eagle. Sometimes I got to see one of them in the hall, but eventually I rarely had contact with them. Finally the counselor arranged a time for me to see my old friend Todd in the library twice during the week, but that actually made me sad. Good friends don't have appointments. They just get together. So this didn't really work out.

During Brenda's time with me, we spent part of the day in the special education class. I would work on assignments from the regular classes. This is where I usually felt most comfortable, but this year it was different. The teacher's special gift was making her students feel worthless, and she found a way to make me feel especially worthless. I thought she was unfair to the students in her class. For example, one time she would not let a boy have cake because he kept making squealing noises. He was just excited and that was how he showed it. The teacher insisted on things being her way. She did not understand people with disabilities, so

her students could not be who they were. Consequently, frustration escalated in her students.

Doing my best to get revenge, I started actually having "accidents" on purpose in my pants. She would get fantastically upset, and I found her anger amusing. She was a special education teacher who I felt had no compassion or understanding for the students or their parents. After I had an accident she would get upset with me, and then I would do it again on purpose. Having those accidents was a way I could control her. One of the times I wet my pants, she suspended me. She called my mom and told her that I was suspended from school for the next day. I would have to miss all of my classes and would receive a zero for the test I had in Global Studies. She did everything she could to prove that she was the one in control.

We had a conference with the teacher and the principal at 7:00 a.m. the Monday after my suspension on Friday. The principal told her that I could take the test and get full credit. Getting revenge was sweet, because she had acted cruelly and unfairly. She really did not belong in special education. Fortunately I was only with her for my two years at the junior high.

Matthew was very successful at the junior high. He was awarded Outstanding Student of the Month in a couple of his classes. He got to attend a breakfast of juice and donuts before school as the reward. Matthew does not like donuts, but of course, he insisted on attending.

His general education teachers were wonderful with him. One time in English he had to write a paper about something that he was good at. Now Matthew did not really have any special skills. He could not do things with his hands very well. That is part of his disability – the hand-eye motor coordination just does not work well for him. I had no idea what he would write about, but he knew. He wrote a two-page paper about how good he was at manipulating people. He wrote about how he would use his behavior to get what he wanted or to show his displeasure for a person. He explained how he would become very vocal, making loud noises, so that his facilitator would take him out of the classroom; he did this if he was not enjoying the teacher's lesson. Also, he wrote that he would purposely bother his aunt by playing with her hair, because he knew it would upset her. If there was a room full of people, he would walk around until he was behind her and put his hand on her hair. The more it seemed to bother her, the more Matthew enjoyed doing it. He did an amazing job on the paper, and it certainly enlightened me about why he did some of the things he did.

The problem we encountered in junior high was his special education teacher. When Matthew was not in regular classes, he would go to the special education room to work at the computer on his homework or to work on life skills activities. His teacher in that classroom just did not get along well with Matt. I'm not sure whether she doubted his intelligence or if it was just one of those personality conflicts. Matthew at that time was not 100% accurate with toileting. Occasionally he did have an accident.

One day I received a phone call at school from his special education teacher. She told me that Matthew was suspended for the next day. I couldn't imagine what he could possibly have done. Being a teacher myself in the same school system, I knew it took a lot for a student to be suspended. She told me that he had an accident in her classroom and had wet his pants. She evidently read him the riot act and so he did it again. She knew he had done it on purpose so she talked to the assistant principal, who happened to be her friend, and they decided to suspend him for the next day. I could not believe my ears. Not only was he being suspended, but he would miss a test in his Global Studies class.

It was a school policy that after students are suspended, they must attend a conference with the school administrator, their parents and the teacher who suspended them. The next Monday morning Mel, Matt, and I went to the school office. The principal, the assistant principal, guidance counselor and the teacher met with us. Needless to say, we were not very happy with the suspension. And for wetting his pants? The principal made it clear that he had not approved the suspension, and he believed that Matthew should not really have been punished in that way. He also said that Matt could take the Global Studies test, and that it would count for full credit. (This was very important to Matthew because at that time he had the highest grade in the class.)

This was only one of the many battles we had with that particular teacher. Later in the year she insisted that he be put in Depends. She could not handle the accidents he occasionally had. The more it bothered her, the more accidents Matthew seemed to have – an example of how he was so good at manipulation. But we finally agreed and sent Depends with him to school.

Matthew started using the toilet less and less. He was regressing. I tried to explain to the teacher that he was depending on the adult diapers. She would not budge. Finally Mel and I met once again with the principal. I had charted the toileting and the data clearly showed that Matt was regressing. The principal agreed that it was doing more harm than good. In order to make peace, he agreed that if Matthew had an accident, he himself, would go down and change Matt. I couldn't believe he would be willing to do that. We told him he should not have to. Any teacher going into teaching severe disabilities special education should know that toileting would be an issue. She should not have such a problem with it. But he agreed to personally take care of it. This principal was another one of those very special people we have encountered. He went way beyond the call of duty to help us in a very frustrating situation. There were times when he did go to the special education room and change Matt, but those times grew fewer and farther between. Matt grew to respect him, and consequently, it became less and less of an issue. I will never forget how kind and helpful he was to us. I can't imagine many principals doing what he did.

CHAPTER 15

My Biggest Battle

Starting as a student at Brownsburg High School was an adventure for a nonverbal autistic boy like my self. This was not only was an adventure; it was definitely a job. The story starts at the junior high. I had competed seventh and eighth grade, and I had received many academic awards that made me feel prepared for high school. As most students feel a bit nervous about the transition to high school, I began to also have some questions about what it would be like as well. Then I ran up against the high school principal. My first encounter with him reminded me of Daniel in the lion's den. The principal was acting as the king who

had made the decree that handicapped students were not allowed to attend Brownsburg High School. They were to attend Pike High School. Pike would take on the duty of educating Brownsburg's handicapped students. I, like Daniel, broke the decree and would have to face the lions. This caused hostility.

My annual case review was held in a stuffy, cramped conference room. When I walked into the room with my aide, the first thing I saw was a group of unfamiliar faces and a couple faces I recognized but did not consider allies. The principal and vice principal from the high school, the counselor, (who happened to be my cousin), and two men from Pike's special education program were all present. Twelve people sat around a huge, polished table that reflected their stern faces. Everyone seemed stone-faced and silent as statues. There was hardly enough room to squeeze in between the chairs and the wall. The walls were white and bare. All I remember is the cold, empty feeling in my stomach. Talk about scared. I was a nervous wreck. I was having a hard time breathing. After seeing all those people and the expressions on their faces, I knew they had already made up their minds.

The conference actually started smoothly. The twelve people each took turns introducing themselves as Mister or Missus So-and-So, each

tagging on their grand titles and credentials, only serving to make me feel insignificant. My special education teacher from the junior high made some derogatory comments because she and I had not really gotten along. First, she had to discuss the so-called accidents I had in her classroom. Then later she explained that I had done well with my regular education classes.

The principal immediately asked, "Do you have any idea how rigorous the curriculum at Brownsburg High School is?" I knew that all he could see in me was a scared, drooling "retarded" boy. He saw what so many people see. So few try to see what is actually inside my heart and my mind. I saw that day that autism was going to be my barrier to enrollment, the same way that race, gender, sexuality or religion can be a barrier for people in so many other facets in life. I was being discriminated against. I decided that I was going to have to fight for my right to get to be a student at BHS.

My parents replied to his question, "Yes, we are very aware of the curriculum. Our older son graduated as valedictorian from Brownsburg." The counselor, my cousin, tried to convince all of the doubters that I did belong at the high school. She was aware of my success thus far. The problem was that she had been a counselor there for only a few months, so her opinion did not seem to count. They didn't want to

listen to anybody. Their minds were made up before the conference even had started.

The two representatives from Pike High School presented special education programs at their school. The presentations made my heart sink. I did not belong in that kind of class, and some of my supporters knew it.

The principal had another question. "When was Matthew last tested?" Someone mentioned my test results from a few years ago, but unfortunately that was not good enough. Most kids never have to go through special testing in order to go to high school. I had done different tests in the past such as the ISTEP (Indiana Statewide Testing for Educational Progress-Plus), and my results were high, but none of this mattered to them. They said I had to be tested again, so my parents agreed, having no other real option.

After testing did not work, the principal stooped to asking, "How can he do PE, swimming especially?" I could not believe it. I wondered to myself, "Can someone actually be so dense? How can he be worried about six weeks of swimming?"

After discussing every asinine issue, something miraculous happened: the principal agreed to enroll me. Thinking back, he probably had no choice. Discrimination is not actually against the law, but I think he knew that

somebody could and would get him on this one. I knew that I was going to have to prove myself to him as well as many others who were equally skeptical.

Academically Matt did a great job in seventh and eighth grade, and he became a better student as far as being able to sit still and listen quietly in class. Then it was over. It was time for his transition to the high school. The spring of his eighth grade year we started the process. We were very concerned about how he would be accepted by the faculty and students. Mel and I were encouraged by the high school administration to look at the special education program at Pike, a nearby school district. This was where all of Brownsburg's special education high school students were sent to school. Brownsburg High School did not have a special education program of its own. So of course, the administrators could not imagine Matthew attending school there.

Mel and I went and observed the Pike program. A young man, about whom we had heard wonderful things, taught there, but the problem was that Matthew did not spend most of his day in special education. He attended three to five regular classes a day. After seeing the Pike program and after a lot of discussion, we decided that we wanted Matthew to go to Brownsburg High School with his classmates and in his community. We received notice that his annual case review had been scheduled. These conferences are always intimidating for parents. Many professionals attend, and they sit across from you at a large table, basically holding your child's future in their hands.

As a teacher, I had sat in on many of my own students' conferences. It is so much different attending as the professional rather than the parent. As a professional, you know that this child will briefly be a part of your life – usually for nine months. If you are a dedicated professional, you want the absolute best for this child. Sure, you are concerned and strive to make the right decisions, but it is so different when you are the parent. First of all, you are usually outnumbered. Many of these professionals act as if they know more than you do, because they hold the degrees in this field. You can be made to feel like you really don't know much, even though you gave birth to this child, cared for him, tended to him each and every day, laid awake night after night crying over the loss of your notion of the perfect child, and met with doctor after doctor and therapist after therapist. You know that your child is a huge part of you and always will be as long as you live, and you would do anything for him. The compassion and understanding of the people at the conference can make all of the difference in your child's life as well as in yours. Compassion and empathy can go a long way, and that is a lesson I have learned through my own experiences as a teacher.

We walked into the conference room at Brownsburg High School on a spring afternoon. I was taken aback and immediately overwhelmed by the number of people sitting in the room. There were four large tables in the room, arranged to form a large square. People were sitting on the outside of the tables so that everyone could face each other. Matthew was sitting with his current facilitator, Brenda. His junior high special education teacher was there along with the high school principal and assistant principal. There were also two gentlemen from Pike High School I was not expecting. There was also a speech therapist and an occupational therapist. We had asked a parent advocate to attend the conference with us, and she was there. Among all of those people sat someone I had no idea would be there: my cousin and another ray of hope, Diane. She would be acting as his high school counselor. I couldn't believe our luck. This was her first year as a high school counselor. The counselors are assigned based on the alphabet – students' last names starting with A-F are assigned one counselor, and so forth. She had not been assigned to Matthew intentionally. He was just in her part of the alphabet! Later I realized that God must have been watching out for us. Diane was such an advocate for Matthew as time went on.

The conference began with Matt's special education teacher giving her report about how Matthew had done at the junior high. She and his facilitator, Brenda, shared how well he had done academically. The therapists shared their annual report. Neither of them had really spent much time with Matthew. We had never even met them before. When we eventually got down to his placement for the following year, the tension in the room grew thick.

The gentlemen from Pike High School told us about their special education program that Brownsburg students were currently attending. We told them that we had observed their program. We also informed them that we preferred to have Matthew attend his "home school" since he would spend a large part of his day attending regular classes. The Brownsburg High School principal began to bristle. He sat up straight and immediately started giving us all of the reasons Matthew should not attend Brownsburg. At one point, he explained that the curriculum at the high school would be much more intense than it had been at the junior high.

The principal made argument after argument, and we refuted each of his reasons why Matthew should go to Pike. Finally he came up with the best reason of all. He asked, "How could Matthew meet his swimming requirement in PE his freshman year?" I thought my husband and I were going to explode either in anger or with laughter. With all of the obstacles facing Matthew, I couldn't believe that was concerned with six weeks of swimming.

The conference went on for a few hours. Matthew sat very patiently at the table, often drooling. I know the administrator looked at Matthew as a poor retarded, drooling youngster who had no place in his school, but he finally conceded. When we left the conference, we were mentally, emotionally and physically exhausted. We had won the battle, but there were going to be many more before we won the war with him.

CHAPTER 16

Proving Myself

The next thing we had to do was find a new facilitator for Matthew. Brenda did not want to go on to the high school with him. The Director of Pupil Services, a former teacher with whom I had taught previously, began the search. It's not easy to find that person who would be just right. First of all, most people don't even know what facilitated communication is. Plus, not many people have worked one on one with a person with autism. It's a lot to ask of anyone. It really takes a special person. The chemistry has to be just right. That person literally becomes Matt's right hand as he types. The two must like and respect each other, and the facilitator must only facilitate – not actually do the typing. There is a very fine line between the two.

The first woman that the director sent out to us had a deformed right hand, meaning that she would have to facilitate with her left hand on Matthew's right hand. That was absolutely not going to work, and it showed me how little the school system understood about the process. It certainly wasn't her fault; she had no idea about what was really required. The search went on for weeks throughout the summer. The fall was drawing close. Finally, a young girl was sent out to meet with us. She had graduated from Brownsburg High School a couple of years previously. She knew the school, many of the staff and was certainly enthusiastic. Nancy Kalina, a trained professional in facilitated communication from the Indiana Resource Center for Autism in Bloomington, Indiana, came several times and worked with her and Matthew. I had some doubts, but she was all we had. It was so scary to think that Matthew's future literally lay in her hands. He was going to have to be able to prove himself to convince the principal and others that he belonged at the high school.

Things started out surprisingly well. Matthew seemed to like her, and he was doing fairly well working with her. Then things began to go downhill. Her notes to me lost their enthusiasm. Matthew was typing that he wasn't getting to say what he wanted, and he was not happy with her. Soon she told me she was going to have to have knee surgery and would not be able to continue working with Matthew. Later I found out that she had been leaving Matt with the nurse and disappearing for long periods of time during the school day. She had quickly lost interest in the job.

My first facilitator was a young girl who had graduated from Brownsburg High School. She was not very good at facilitating. She was also not a very responsible person. She did not do her job well. Consequently, I had real problems doing my best typing. We really did not do well together. She finally found an excuse to quit, and I was so happy that she did. I hoped for a new facilitator who would find the facilitating easier. A lot of teachers did not believe I could do the work, but I was ready to prove myself. Because I had no facilitator at school, my mother did all of my homework and tests with me, but that made the teachers think my mom was doing the work. I did not have the chance to show them what I really could do.

Since Matthew did not have a facilitator, an aide in the high school would take him to his classes and write down his assignments. She would send them home, and I would work with him every evening until the homework was done. I had started helping out with unfinished homework since he was in third grade. However, now I had all of it to do. We would do homework in the car on the way to soccer games, at half-time during soccer games and usually on the way home. I would usually read the material to him. He would type on his Alpha Smart, a small keyboard with a very small screen. The Alpha Smart would save the files, and then we would hook it up to the printer at home and print out the work. We had to be creative in using our time, because I still had my papers to grade.

I received a call that the Director of Pupil Services had found a new facilitator. She had spent the last few days with Matt and was interested in the job. I immediately called Nancy to see if she could come up and help me train another facilitator for Matt. She came to the high school several times. I could tell she had her doubts about this woman. She stayed after school one day and held a small meeting with his new facilitator and a small group of interested teachers. I finally got to meet this woman who would hopefully be instrumental in Matt's success. She was from the Philippines and spoke English but not fluently. My internal warning signals started buzzing immediately, but I knew that she was only going to be hired on a temporary basis.

Finally the principal hired a lady from the Philippines to be my new assistant. She was an undereducated woman and did not really seem to have a desire to learn how to type with me. I could not get any of the answers I wanted to say. As a new facilitator, she needed more training. We went to a conference and met with a woman from Syracuse University in New York who was an expert in FC. The new facilitator worked with me, and the expert watched and

gave suggestions. I was worried because I knew my new facilitator was not really concerned at all about improving her typing with me.

A lady who was an expert in the field of facilitated communication from Syracuse University was going to hold a small conference in Bloomington, Indiana. Matthew, his dad, and I planned to attend. I invited Matt's new facilitator to go with us. It was on a Saturday in October. She agreed to go if she was reimbursed for her time and mileage, which was, of course, fair. At the end of the conference she gave me her itemized bill with hours and mileage. I knew right then and there that it was just going to be a job to her, and that her heart was not fully in it. Everyone should be compensated for their work and time, but this is a job that requires more care than this woman was willing to invest.

Problems developed almost immediately. Matthew was failing easy quizzes and tests on material that I knew he understood. Matt was not getting to type what he wanted to say; his facilitator was having trouble even after the training. Matthew grew increasingly frustrated with this facilitator and started having some behavior issues. I cannot imagine what it was like for him to have so much knowledge and not be able to communicate it. He could share what he knew only with the assistance of a skilled facilitator.

I continued to look for a facilitator for Matt on my own. I found a parent of a little boy with special needs in my school. She was working in the cafeteria at that time. We talked quite a bit about Matthew and about being a facilitator. She came to our house to watch Matt type, and she was very interested in him and the job. I called the principal and told him all about her. He said he would call her, and after a few days of not hearing back from him, I called him. He said he had interviewed her, but that she would just not work out, but he could not give me a reason why. I was so disappointed. He just said to trust him.

Finally I got a call from the principal saying he was going to hire the temporary facilitator, who was still working with Matthew, on a permanent basis. I told him I wanted to meet with him first. One morning before school started, I went to the high school. The Director of Pupil Services was there as well as the principal, assistant principal and counselor. I pleaded with the principal not to hire her. I explained to him that she was not working out. Matthew was terribly frustrated because she was the one doing the typing, not him. I always hated it when my eyes got teary, my voice cracked and I knew I was on the verge of crying. I wanted to appear so strong, but my heart was breaking. I knew this would be a disaster. Nothing I said could change his mind. The facilitator was going to be hired, and they would no longer look for another one.

It wasn't long after our meeting that Matthew was suspended from school for one day. I was told that a special education teacher suspended him because he would not type with his facilitator in the Life Skills class. I couldn't blame Matthew – he refused to type because she was not letting him type what he wanted to say. This took place in the last ten minutes of the last period of the school day. I could not believe that a teacher in special education, who is supposed to have the training and understanding in dealing with special needs students, would suspend him for such a thing. I had to take the next day off from teaching so I could spend the day with him at home due to his suspension.

As my new facilitator and I worked together, things went from bad to worse. I was failing tests when I should have gotten A's. With her facilitating, I could not type the answers I wanted. She took my hand and pulled it to the wrong keys. Finally I really got upset and refused to type anymore with her, so the teacher of the class suspended me from school for the next day, and the administration supported her decision; they had no idea that they had hired an incompetent facilitator. They made their own decisions about my future.

She did not even try to improve her facilitation. During that time I was angry and worried about what was going to happen with my education. I wanted the school to know I belonged there, but without a good facilitator I could not prove anything. One day during Christmas vacation, the lady called my mother and said she had fallen on the ice and had broken her ankle; she would not be coming back

to school. I was sad for her, but I was so happy for me that I could have screamed. Now there was hope that we might find another facilitator who could help me show the principal and everyone else that I could do the work.

CHAPTER 17

God Hears Our Prayers

A woman named Kriss had been volunteering at the high school. I really liked her. She helped the teacher who worked with the kids who had learning disabilities. When the other facilitator did not come back to school in January, the teacher asked Kriss if she would be interested in working with me. She said yes hoping that she could learn how to facilitate. Once again Nancy Kalina came and got Kriss started on learning how to facilitate. Kriss wanted to learn, and she worked hard, trying to facilitate the correct way.

Immediately after Christmas, Judy Clark, a teacher from the high school called me. Mrs. Clark taught students with learning disabilities. She had been put in charge of Matt's educational plan and was to help make sure it was carried out appropriately. Mrs. Clark knew a woman named Kriss, a parent of a high school student, and she was doing volunteer work in her classroom. She and her family were new to Brownsburg. She said that Kriss had met Matthew and had really bonded with him. She was possibly interested in working as Matt's facilitator. When I met her, I liked her immediately and could tell she was an intelligent, caring woman.

I was so excited about this woman. I really got my hopes up. The best thing was that she believed it was really me doing the typing. I wanted her to work out so much. This was exactly what I had prayed for. With her, maybe I could show everybody that I did have what it took to be at BHS. We just had to learn to work together.

At first we just worked on set work, meaning that we were answering a lot of easy questions that we both knew the answers to. The purpose was for Kriss to get the feel of FC. She got used to resisting as my hand had to push forward leading hers. That is the most important part of facilitating. She was a super fast learner. Nancy Kalina came and worked with Kriss and me under the supervision of the school. We

worked hard and it really helped. Soon I was getting to type open-ended answers with Kriss.

Then it was time for the semester tests. With the facilitator being new, I wanted my mom to facilitate with me on the tests. The teachers said no so I just refused to take the tests. Everybody else got to take the tests without a disadvantage, so why couldn't I? I did end up taking a test with my mom facilitating, but she had to come to school and take it. Kriss watched my mom and me work together to take the test and learned the techniques my mom used.

Final exams were coming up soon. Kriss had not had the training or experience to take the final exams with Matt. The school would not let me facilitate with Matthew on his semester tests. Nancy Kalina, who had trained with Kriss and the other facilitators, said she would come up from Bloomington and take the tests with Matt. The first test was scheduled for the next day. Matthew refused to do the test with her. Nothing she could say or do would change his mind. He just sat there so, of course, he failed his exam. I cried. I talked and pleaded with Matthew. I just couldn't figure out why he was doing this. After all the frustrations of the first semester, now we had a potentially good facilitator, and he refused to take the finals. All I could figure out was that he lacked confidence in Kriss because she had just started facilitating with him.

Finally the school decided that I could do the English exam with Matt if I came to school and we had a proctor. Kriss was the proctor. I went to school with Matt at 7:00 a.m., and Kriss watched me facilitate with Matthew as he took the English final. She was so attentive, and she told me later that watching me work with Matt really helped her. She had a lot of good questions. I was so impressed with her.

CHAPTER 18

My Special Angel

Soon I started doing the majority of my work with Kriss at school. She was a fast student with FC. After a few weeks we were much better facilitating together. Kriss wanted me to do the typing, not her. She wanted to make sure I was getting to say what I wanted to say. I appreciated that very much. She was possibly the best facilitator I have ever had.

The student is worth only the skill of the facilitator. I had to be able to type just what I wanted to say. More than once I tested her by typing the wrong answer to an obviously easy question just to see if she would let me type the answer I wanted even though she knew it was wrong. I felt better knowing that she was typing my answers and not the answers she thought were right. This is the most important thing about facilitated communication. It only works if the facilitator truly allows the individual to do the typing.

It was stupid of me to treat her so badly. She was the best thing that had happened to me since elementary school, but when I got upset, I took it out on Kriss. I couldn't yell or complain to express anger or frustration, so I acted terribly with Kriss. The things that I did to her I don't want to even tell. I was ashamed of them then and to tell them now makes me feel bad. I got so angry that one time I tore her sweater. She could have quit, but she didn't, and this told me just how dedicated she was to me. She had such devotion and patience, but she would sometimes get angry right back. Then I would apologize and things would be okay again. I had so much respect for her. I will love her always. The best thing she ever did was tell me that she would stay with me until I graduated from high school. That was at the end of my freshman year. And she kept her word. She did stay with me.

At the end of each day Kriss and I would go down to the Cross Category room. That was nice for me because we relaxed and I could be myself. The Cross Category room was for special

education students who all had some type of handicap. They always were glad to see us, and I got a warm welcome from everyone, students and adults. I could relax and be myself, and no one cared. I could rock and spin in circles and act autistic, and that was just fine. In regular classes I did as best as I could to blend in with normal students. That was always difficult because my brain wanted to act autistic.

In my mind I want to be normal and be like everyone else, but an autistic student is not like everyone else. I have this very strong desire to spin sometimes. It feels comforting to me, as does rocking back and forth. Sitting in class could be so exhausting for me. Sometimes sitting still really was a challenge; sometimes it is more difficult than the work itself.

The second semester began. Kriss went to classes with Matt, took notes and started facilitating his homework with him at school during his scheduled study halls. Matt was only taking three of four classes because it took him so long to do the work for each class. The homework he could not finish at school was sent home for me to finish with him. It meant a lot of work in the evenings, but I was already used to that from the first semester. Matt seemed to love Kriss and told me that she was learning how to facilitate quickly. He seemed pleased, and that, of course, made me feel good.

Kriss had never really worked with anyone with a disability, but some how, some way, she and Matthew connected from the beginning. Just when we had been absolutely desperate for a good facilitator, Kriss and her family moved to town. It was like she appeared from nowhere at the very moment things seemed totally hopeless, as if God knew that she was who Matthew needed at that moment. She was definitely an answer to many, many prayers.

After facilitating with Matt for four and a half years, she walked across the stage with him to get his diploma. She still works at the high school today, assisting many other students with different types of disabilities. I don't think she realized how gifted she was and still is in that particular field. Working with Matthew was the beginning of her new career – and she is exceptional at her job. So many other students have been lucky enough to have Kriss working alongside them, benefiting from her patience, kindness, and understanding. She has a special talent that few other people have. Matthew owes his success at the high school to Kriss. She was God's ray of light, and she helped Matt to bloom.

CHAPTER 19

Bad Days

Having a good, willing facilitator was such a relief. However, the problems were far from over. Matt was taking PE the second semester and had swimming for six weeks. He did not like to get in the pool and would not get in because the water was notorious for being cold. I finally suggested having a couple of boys gently push or drop him into the water. This worked for a while. Then I received a phone call from the assistant principal that Matt was not cooperating in swimming. He would urinate on the side of the pool. If it only happened once, it might have been an accident, but it seemed to be happening frequently. I asked the assistant principal what the teacher was doing with Matt once he got into the water and found that basically Matt was just left standing there shivering. I told him that it was no wonder Matt didn't want to get into the pool if he was just going to stand there and be cold. The problem was, of course, that Matt had to complete the swimming course requirement.

Also, at the beginning of the school year, everyone had been trying to work out how Matt would get changed for swimming when he had a female assistant. She obviously could not go into the boys' dressing room, and Matt sure couldn't go into the girls'. One of the male PE teachers was asked if he would help with it. His reply was "Are you kidding? I don't get paid enough for that!" That comment really hurt.

Matt and the school survived swimming, but it was definitely one day at a time. Looking back, it seems so trite in the grand scheme of things that my son, diagnosed early in life as severely mentally handicapped, would encounter so many issues over a six week swimming class, when he was successfully attending algebra and biology classes and was actually doing excellent work. I never could figure out the big deal. I always thought that if the people making Matt's success so difficult could live a month in our shoes, they would certainly have looked at his educational concerns differently.

One day a teacher, who had never really had any experience with students with autism, called very concerned because she though Matt was giving her "the finger" in class. Matt would take his middle finger of his left hand and rub up along the side of his nose. Matt had done that for years – it was just one of his little movements or quirks that we all have. I told her I wished that Matt had the dexterity and fine motor control to do it on purpose. It was not within his realm of motor control to intentionally stick his middle finger up.

This was a very difficult year for Matt, Mel, his new facilitator, his teachers, the administration and me. To my knowledge, Matthew was the first severely disabled student Brownsburg High School had ever enrolled, and they did not know what to make of his obstinate and sometimes defiant behavior. I had learned years ago that when push comes to shove, Matthew wins. He cannot be forced or threatened to do what he does not want to do. However, high school teachers and principals do not accept that. Often the theory is that you can't give in to a student. If you did, you would lose your sense of authority and control. But Matthew, like many children with autism, was different. Their brains do not work like most kids' brains. The "if you do this, then you can do that" never worked with Matt. Overall, the school system was trying to make a difficult situation work. I had had fourteen years with Matthew; they had only had a few months. We all had a lot to learn.

That year I received several phone calls from the high school during my days at school. The secretary would come on the intercom in my classroom, and I would immediately get a sick feeling in my stomach. I would have to have an aide cover my class while I went and talked to whoever had called me this time. There were so many days that I would have to dry my eyes quickly before returning to my own classroom. Luckily I had a very kind and supportive principal in my building. There were more than a few times when I would have to leave during my prep time and run to the high school for one crisis or another.

Matthew finished his first year of high school with good grades and a facilitator who could type with him and who let him say what he wanted to say. There were many ups and downs during that first year – probably more downs than ups. But the year ended with the best news I had heard in a long time. Kriss told me that she planned to stay with Matthew until he graduated, but knowing that she and her husband had frequently moved because of his job, I didn't want to get my hopes up. It would mean at least four more years of high school. Since Matthew could only take about four classes each semester, due to the slowness of his typing, he would need a fifth year to complete all of the requirements. In spite of my skepticism, I was still excited. She had worked out well, and if she did stay, I would not have to go through another summer searching for and training a new facilitator and that was a huge relief.

We spent the summer going to Kings Island, watching Katy play soccer, and just doing family things. It was so nice to just be able to relax, knowing Matt was set for the next school year. Too soon, summer came to a close, and it was back to school. Matt's second year of high school started off well. He liked his teachers and everything seemed to be moving along just fine, but suddenly he started having behavior problems. He would be walking in the hall with Kriss on his way to class and just stop. He would stand in the middle of the hall and refuse to move. Other times he would refuse to work on an assignment with Kriss, and there were days he would just refuse to take a test.

When he had a bad day, I would sit down with him at the computer in the evening and ask him what was wrong. Sometimes he would not type anything; other times, he typed that he wanted to have some friends. It was always the same. "If I could talk, I would be able to have friends." That was always the hard one to deal with. He was probably right. Many of the kids were nice to him but were not "friends" with him. My heart always seemed to tear a little bit more when he typed things like that. However, I would try to remind him of the things he had to be thankful for, and I constantly reminded him of his goal to graduate from high school. I would tell him how he and Kriss would some day walk across that platform in the gym, and he would get his diploma from his principal, the man who didn't think he belonged there. It was always hard to find the words to both console and encourage him.

I just never saw any rhyme or reason for Matthew's behavior, and I still don't. Even though he can type with me, there is still a wall there. Sometimes I don't feel like I am getting completely honest answers from him. Sometimes I think he types what he thinks I want to hear. To this day, there are so many times I just want to be able to break through the wall and carry on a verbal conversation with him. I want to talk with him. I never could understand why he would intentionally fail a test. I would ask him, "What do you think you are going to accomplish?" It's like he was playing mind games with me.

Sometimes he would call Kriss names and tell her he wanted her to quit so he could stay home with me, even though he knew that was not an option. Kriss always sent his assignments home with him along with a note about his day. Eventually I dreaded going home at the end of my school day, afraid to see what kind of day Matt had had. Did he do his work? Did he even go to class? My mood always hinged and still does on what kind of day Matthew has had. If he worked hard and I got a good note, I felt such a relief. But if he had had one of his frequent bad days, I would be upset the rest of the evening.

There were several times when he would eventually type, after a bad spell of bad behavior and obstinacy, "Well, I got your attention." When I thought things were going fine, his behavior would take a turn for the worse, and I would go down to the computer with him to try and find out what was bothering him. I honestly think sometimes he just enjoyed my attention and being able to manipulate and control me as well as others.

Being nonverbal, one has very little power or control over other people. When I am angry or upset, I can talk or yell or communicate in a number of ways how I'm feeling. But Matthew can't do that, except when he has someone to type with at the computer. His control and power over others frequently can come through his behavior. So many times I never could figure out what was bothering him or why he was acting like he was. Maybe sometimes he didn't really know himself. We all have our off days.

One day I got a note from Kriss about how he refused to get off the bus at school that morning. No one could get him to stand up – not the aide on the bus or the driver. Finally they called the school security officer. Come to find out, no one had unbuckled his seat belt. He had sat there, getting verbally scolded and pulled by the arm and had no way to tell anyone or indicate that his seat belt was still on. I can't imagine the frustration and humiliation he must have felt.

CHAPTER 20

Seizures

During Matt's high school years, when he was about seventeen, he started having seizures. He had had them earlier in his life, but they had been controllable by medication. There were so many mornings I would practically carry him out to the bus because he had had a seizure right before the bus came. Sometimes he would have them in class. The seizures were just one more problem for Matthew, but he has managed to work through this and so many other hurdles.

Seizures are a nightmare. They started when I was about five or six. We could not control them. When I first discovered that they

start as a short act of brain failure, that scared me. I would be right side up and then find myself on the floor. Seizures do not give you much warning. They just knock you over like the feeling you get when a doctor gives you some bad news. It's an intense jolt to your body. Some of the seizures I have instantly knock me hard to the ground.

Eventually they got so bad I had to wear a helmet for protection. I hated that so much. It really didn't help stop the seizures of course, but having it on protected my brain in case of a fall. After the seizures were under control by medication, the helmet had no use. I completely stopped having them, but I continued taking medication. Then when I was about sixteen, the seizures began to haunt me again. I began feeling like I was getting light-headed, and I felt I could fall over. Then I would fall back into the wall. The seizures grew in intensity, but I didn't learn until later just how intense they could be.

Over the years I have been to several neurologists. They tried to help me, but no one has really been successful. I have met unique people however. This one woman doctor specializing in neurology had an unusual appearance but was highly recommended. She had black hair that hung down her back, and she wore black lipstick too. Usually she wore long black sweaters, short skirts and black boots. There were old

recliners in the rooms where she examined the patients. She really scared my mom, but I liked her. She wasn't able to help me though. She tried lots of different medications, but no medicine stopped the seizures. Finally she sent us to the neurologist she had trained with. The neurologist was Italian. I didn't care where she was from as long as she could help me. She spoke with an accent, and every time that she ended a sentence, she would go, "Huh?" This got on my mom's nerves. She actually did help my seizures for a while though.

Right now I have a vegus nerve stimulator embedded in my chest. This sends electrical impulses to my brain. In some cases people can be free from seizures. I still have them but less frequently. I hope that someday they will be gone forever.

Matt's seizures have also led to some interesting predicaments. Josh worked for a provider agency and often took Matthew places in the community. He had taken Matthew to a nearby shopping mall. This mall was not in the best area and was rather known for its high crime rate. However, it was broad daylight on a sunny, summer afternoon, and it was the closest mall to our home. When Josh and Matt got home, Josh told us that Matt had had a seizure. It occurred in the mall parking lot. When Matt fell backwards, he bumped into the car next to Josh's, setting off the burglar alarm.

When I finally quit laughing, I asked Josh how long the alarm lasted. He didn't know. He got Matt in the car and took off as quickly as possible.

Another time we were at a Colts' game. We had invited a good friend of mine to go with us. Everything went well until the game ended. We were leaving the stadium amidst the crowd rushing to their cars. Matt had a seizure right at the top of the stairs leading to the sidewalk. Boom – he just went down. Instantly there were at least three police officers and security guards there to help us. They were so nice. We just gently pulled Matt out of the main stream of people until he regained his bearings.

The scariest incident with seizures happened at the Fort Myers airport. We had flown from Indianapolis to Washington D.C., and we were changing planes to go on to Fort Myers. We had not flown for many years, but the first part of our flight had gone very well. After a brief layover in Washington, we boarded the next plane. We were not seated together on this leg of our journey. Matt, Katy and I ended up together in the last row of seats, and Mel was seated about ten rows ahead of us. Matt had seizures, one after another, the whole trip to Fort Myers. It started as we boarded the plane, and he fell into a lady's lap. We had recently changed medications, and they obviously were not working. He had never had seizures that continued one after another after another. There was absolutely nothing I could do. When we finally landed at Fort Myers, I told Mel what was going on. He asked me about getting a wheelchair, but not wanting to create a scene, I said no. We started down the escalator to Baggage Claim. Katy was in front of us, and Mel and I were on each side of Matthew. About four or five steps from the bottom, Matt dropped down with a seizure. The steps kept moving, and Mel and I were trying to lift him up, but falling all over the place as the steps moved downward. I'm sure it was only a matter of seconds, but it seemed an eternity. As soon as Katy got on solid ground, she lifted Matt's legs, and we got him off the escalator. Out of nowhere, three or four security guards appeared to help us. They were there before I even had a chance to look up. We looked Matthew over for cuts and bruises. He had some scrapes, but overall, the injuries were minor. One of the security officers brought a wheelchair over, and we got Matthew into it. They offered to call an ambulance, but we declined. I had to fill out an accident report while Mel went to get our rental car. The officers helped load our luggage into the trunk. They could not have been nicer or more helpful. Eventually we ended up in the emergency room in order to get the seizures to stop.

CHAPTER 21

People in My Life at BHS

During high school I had some interesting teachers, one of whom took charge of my individualized education plan (IEP). Having students with learning disabilities did not prepare Mrs. Clark for me. It was a very disappointing relationship at the beginning. She just did not understand facilitated communication. In time she developed a better understanding, especially when Kriss came. I started doing my English classes with Mrs. Clark, because her class was small. This gave me a chance for more social interaction. When my classmates had free time during the period, they would ask me questions, and I would get time to respond by typing. Mrs. Clark was so

nice to me. The relationship had a rough start but turned out very well.

My algebra teacher was a strange guy with wild eyebrows and hair. He was really the best math teacher I ever had. The kids enjoyed getting him to tell them stories to keep from doing algebra, but he found time to tell stories and still teach the math. The only bad thing about him was that he didn't really understand my disability. He thought that I was trying to be disruptive when I had problems sitting still or being quiet, and once he suspended me. Suspending me really took a lot of nerve, but he did it anyway. I forgave him because of his lack of understanding my disability, but the fact that he suspended me changed my feelings about him.

Mr. Downey, the speech teacher, was better by far. The speech requirement had everyone stumped. How could a nonverbal student take speech? Mr. Downey had the answer. He suggested that I write what I wanted him to say. He was going to give my speeches orally for me. I had to write directions for how I wanted him to say it. For example, I would tell him if I wanted the speech to be serious or humorous. I had so much fun that semester. My favorite speech was about the Hindenburg exploding. I was so happy when the principal came to observe that class. Mr. Downey gave my speech as

Big John, the eyewitness reporter. The whole class liked it, and so did my principal. He got to see and hear how much I really did belong in his school.

I had really done most of my speeches with my mom. Doing them with her always seemed easier, and she spent more time with me at the computer. I enjoyed the time when we were all alone working together. The next speech was about whether this little Cuban boy who stole into the U.S. should be allowed to stay, and Mr. Downey decided that I should do it with Kriss. She did not mind, but I did mind. It made me mad that I couldn't do it with my mom. He said I had to do it with Kriss or get an F. Giving me the ultimatum made me more determined not to give him the satisfaction of getting his way. I got the F, but eventually he gave in and let me make the grade up on the next speech as long as I did part of it with Kriss at school.

I also had Mr. Downey for Theatre Arts. One time he had me dress up like Bob Barker. I was the head of the production company for the Price is Right, my favorite show. I wore a suit to school. The women said I looked "hot" in my suit!

Another time Mr. Downey had me write a speech about the highs and lows of my life. Then he had me sit on the stage, and he sat next to me. I rock back and forth a lot due to my

autism. Mr. Downey sat beside me and rocked in rhythm with me. A few moments passed, and then Mr. Downey moved out from me as if he was leaving my body. He gave my speech the way I would have if I could, then he came and sat back down beside me. He was so wonderful. The class loved the speech, and I will never forget it.

During my high school years, Katy was going to a church group for teenagers called Christians Having an Outreach Service (CHAOS). It met on Sunday mornings in a building near the church, since there wasn't enough room in the church. The kids were mostly from my high school. Many of them told Katy they knew me from Mr. Downey's speech class. Katy thought I should attend the service too. She thought that if I went to school with them, I should go to church with them. The youth minister was great and so funny. With Katy's encouragement, I started attending regularly. Katy and I were both baptized the same morning. The minister had to pick me up and dunk me because I have a fear of leaning back in the water. I had talked to him earlier and told him to do what it took.

CHAPTER 22

Graduation Arrives

It was finally time to graduate. It was the goal I had had in my mind since going to regular classes in third grade. I had dreamed of this night for so long, but at the same time I kind of felt like it might never really happen. Kriss thought I could do it, but I was not as confident. I had only hoped she was right. Giving up this dream had crossed my mind a few times, but Kriss never let me. She did all that she could to keep me going. If Kriss had not continued to give her best, I would have never made it.

The time came when I received my cap and gown. I will never forget the good feeling I had when I put them on. I had rehearsal Friday morning for about two hours. The kids were so excited, but I don't think anyone was more excited than I was. Most of the kids had always known they would graduate someday, but for me it was an impossible dream come true. I couldn't have imagined all those years before that I would graduate from high school with some of the same kids who actually helped me in third grade. That day was the best one of my life at that point. When a student graduates, the parents are so proud, but I think my parents were the proudest parents there. We had all realized that a dream was coming true – a dream that had given us hope for my future.

Kriss and I walked in together wearing our caps and gowns. She wore them so she would not be obvious as she sat with all of the graduates and me. I had to really focus on sitting still and being quiet. The speeches seemed endless but finally they were over, and the time came for me to get my diploma. I didn't just walk across the stage. I galloped and jumped. I was so excited that I couldn't help it. At the end of graduation, my family was hugging and kissing me. Was I ever proud! All I could wish for had actually happened. I had written Kriss a letter as a way to say all the things I would like to have spoken to her. After the crowd started leaving I gave the letter and a gift to Kriss. We sat on the bleachers, and she read the letter. She

started crying and hugged me. She even kissed me, something she had never done. She opened my gift. I had gotten her a bracelet with a gold heart that had "Love, Matt" engraved on it. Graduation was great, but the open house the next day was unbelievably good too. The people just kept coming and coming.

Graduation from high school had been THE goal for the last ten years of our lives. Now, all of a sudden, it was here. The hours and hours we spent at the computer had all been worth it. Our son was going to walk across the stage of Brownsburg High School in his cap and gown. Words cannot express how unbelievably proud we were. My dad had passed away when Matt was four. I wanted to tell him so badly about Matthew's accomplishment. He never would have believed it.

When I got home from school on the day of his graduation, Matt was sprawled out on his bedroom floor sound asleep. I could hardly contain myself throughout the day, and here he was, sound asleep. I instantly started worrying about when he had gone to the bathroom. He still had occasional accidents. I knew graduation would be a long ceremony, and he sure couldn't get up to go to the restroom. (To this day, our lives often revolve around Matt's bathroom schedule.)

Graduation brought an absolute flood of emotions: happiness, pride and elation, but also a great sadness and fear. Kriss, Matt's right hand for the last four and a half years, was not going on to college with him. Those years of having a wonderful facilitator and a faithful friend were coming to an end. She was a special person. I know God had sent her to us when we had been most desperate. She was another of our many blessings.

During the ceremony I watched Kriss as she lovingly straightened Matt's cap on his head. He looked up at her with his big, brown eyes. Tears flowed from my eyes as I watched them together. I thought back to all of the good days and the bad days. I never had really thought Kriss would survive four and a half years with Matt. I know it wasn't easy for her, but they had formed a special bond that few people understood. In a note to Matthew, Kriss had once written:

> I knew it was you when you grabbed my hand and started to type with a passion and didn't stop until you said all you had to say. You told me exactly what you thought about certain things, your feelings, what made you happy and what made you sad. And when I asked your mom about some of the things, and her response was the same as what you told me, I knew from then on you trusted me to facilitate your thoughts into words, and it was truly you.

We had already been hunting for the next facilitator. We knew, as in the past, this person would be the essential ingredient to Matt's success. In the last couple of weeks, we thought we had found just the right person. She had known Matthew for several months, and their relationship seemed to click.

She attended Matt's graduation. At the end of the ceremony, I took a picture of her with Kriss and Matt. The picture was of Matt, his past and his future.

Worrying was temporarily put aside the next day as we had a house full of company who had come to celebrate Matt's accomplishments with us. Mrs. Kilian, his third grade teacher, and many others from school had come to congratulate him. During the weekend I watched our video of graduation over and over again. It was such a happy moment in time. But I wondered what the future would bring.

CHAPTER 23

My First Years in College

Getting into college proved to be far easier for Matt than getting into our own public high school. We filled out an application with his grade point average and all sorts of other information. He had no extra curricular activities, no summer jobs, or anything like that. However, he was applying to Indiana University Purdue University of Indianapolis (IUPUI). The requirements at this school were not as stringent as they were for many private colleges. Many of the students there worked during the day and took classes at night, and many were adults wishing to further their education. Grades from high school and motivation were the predominant requirements. Matthew was admitted with no questions asked.

We soon discovered that the university had an Adaptive Education Department. I called and talked to a man named Tim Anno who worked in that area. He was most helpful and understanding as I explained Matthew's history and disability. Tim was very encouraging and supportive. One of the main concerns was how Matt would use the restroom with a female facilitator. At the high school he had gone to the nurse's clinic. Tim suggested that his facilitator carry a sign made on a standard sized piece of paper that said, "Temporarily Closed." She could hang it on the women's door when Matt needed to use the bathroom on campus. It was a simple solution to an interesting dilemma.

I began my college classes the August after I graduated from high school. I was scared to death. Going to college was not what I had hoped it would be. I had really wanted to go away to college. However, living at home and going to school during the day proved to be the best plan for me. I had to go to orientation and meet with my advisor who would help enroll me in classes. She was a kind, white-haired lady named Mrs. DeLong. We also met with a special needs advisor named Tim Anno. His job was to help make the professors aware of any modifications I would need.

I had a new facilitator. She had stayed with me after school my senior year of high school. I liked her a lot and thought that she

would be a good facilitator for me, but after two or three months, I realized that she was taking some pain medicine that affected her ability to think clearly. I had enrolled in an easy math class so she could learn to facilitate easier; Math is the most difficult subject to do on a computer. I knew how to do the problems, but she sometimes would type what she thought was right. She moved my hand where she wanted it to go, a problem that was all too familiar.

Consequently, I failed a test. My mom knew that I could do the algebra. My mom was allowed to do the next test with me. I ended up with a B in the class, and that facilitator quit, knowing that she was not able to successfully facilitate. Even though I was relieved that she quit, the feeling of sadness was also there. I liked her so much, but she had not been able to do the job as successfully as I had hoped.

The second semester was better. My mom did two classes with me online, and they went well. The best class was English Composition. The class divided into groups. We had a writing assignment, and then we sent a copy of our paper to each group member. We would meet online to discuss each other's papers. I liked that because I could type my comments just as the others in my group typed theirs. This was the first time I felt that we were all equal. Each

writing assignment helped my desire to write my life story. I found that writing really was therapeutic for me. It gave me the chance to put my feelings out there on the surface for others to see and possibly understand. I enjoy letting the world get to know me and others like me.

Since we didn't have a facilitator for the second semester, I took two online classes with Matt. I would teach all day, come home, throw down my coat, and we would get started. Mel soon learned to cook and clean up the kitchen. Sometimes he would do the reading with Matthew, and I could do other things. After Matt went to bed, I would grade papers and do my own schoolwork. It was a difficult time, but Matt was willing to work so hard. I knew I could as well.

Raising a handicapped child requires much more time and attention for that child. So many times I feel like I have sacrificed time with Katy and Joey because of all of the time spent with Matt. I have missed several soccer games, band concerts and other activities because I was home working with Matt on his schoolwork. I had to work hard to balance my time; it took some major juggling, but I think we made it work. I hope Joey and Katy never felt neglected. I'm sure there were brief moments when they did, but I never wanted them to feel second to Matthew in any way. I do hope they saw the love and devotion that it takes to raise children. Good children become good adults. It takes much time and commitment, regardless of the circumstances.

One of Matt's classes that semester was English Composition. He had a wonderful professor who enjoyed Matt's writing. He had to write a paper about a controversial issue, so he chose facilitated communication. That paper was the beginning of Matt's desire to write a book. The professor strongly encouraged Matt to try and get something published someday.

CHAPTER 24

Praise the Lord

After I had started college, I had the great opportunity to go to my first Handycamp, and it has become one of the best things in my life. Handycamp is a camp for adults with disabilities, sponsored by Lutheran Disabilities Ministry. The camps are held at different locations during the summer, and each camp lasts about five days. All campers have companions who help them get dressed, shower and have fun. These companions are good, kind volunteers, many of whom come from church groups. They are usually high school or college kids, but some are adults. The campers stay in

cabins and sleep in bunk beds; for our protection, we get the bottom bunk, and the companion gets the top. We are actually treated like royalty.

The companionship is the best part. I had wanted to have good friends for a long time. I have had the chance to make some at camp, including Luke and Matt. They both email me occasionally during the year. They give me that sense of friendship I always wanted but never really had.

There are so many fun activities at camp as well. The days start out with a breakfast of bacon, sausage, scrambled eggs and pancakes. We have Bible Study and sing songs praising God. Then we do crafts and build wooden things that relate to our camp theme. We also do lots of outdoor activities. The favorite among campers is swimming but usually with the water being cold, I stay at camp.

Camp gives me a chance to just be the autistic person I am, and I am accepted. Because of my disability and because I am nonverbal, there are few chances in my life to form real friendships, but I am able to do that at camp. When I am there, everybody reaches out to me. They do their best to talk to me even though I can't respond. Everybody has fun being together and singing for God. I give my thanks to God for this terrific opportunity. I have had many

firsts at camp, including dancing. I had never gone to a dance, until attending Handycamp. Dances have given me a chance to feel like a normal teenager, even though I am past that time in my life. I missed things like dances in high school.

I think that all disabled people should have the chance to go to a camp that welcomes anybody who is different like me. I have had God in my heart with me for the majority of my life, but going to Handycamp has done so much to strengthen my faith. I have seen the glory of God and His grace at camp. The sweetness of our singing and praying together is evidence of God's love for us all.

My faith determines who I am. It has given my life meaning. I feel that God creates human beings for some purpose, and I believe that my purpose is to help others derive empathy for people with disabilities. I have found hope in a hopeless situation. God has given me the chance to write this book when at first I was thought to be severely mentally disabled. The article that my grandmother found in the newspaper about Laura Poorman, her student Seth and facilitated communication was part of God's scheme. My mom didn't look at it for months. She had doubts, but finally called the school where Poorman taught. All of this had to be part of God's plan. There were so many

things that happened, so that I would be found in this body. I strongly believe that God was using this time to discover me. The fact that I had to facilitate in order to be found makes my story a miracle. I think God is very near to each of us, but He works in His time. God gives us all better lives if we do the best we can with His gifts.

I now also belong to a Bible study group in my church. The members are either disabled in some way or are caregivers for someone who is. We have been together about four years now. This group of people has given love a new meaning for me. They welcomed me and my mother into their group. They accept me for who I am. They understand what the word "disability" means. I thank God for them and their love.

CHAPTER 25

God Does It Again

In the summer of 2005, we started another search for a good facilitator. Sycamore, an agency that helps provide me with services, found Carla. She had stayed with me a couple of times and knew a little bit about me. Carla was interested in taking the job. Once again Kriss helped train this new facilitator. Carla was very smart and learned really quickly. I liked her instantly. She was so determined to facilitate what I wanted to say. We started the fall semester with two classes. One was on campus and the other online. The semester went well. Carla does a good job, and you can't do much to anger her. Sometimes I find words coming from my finger that are not very nice. I do this when I hope to upset her. I do this when I want to stop working and sometimes just for fun. The funny thing about Carla is that she can get as mean as I can when she wants to! I like that about her. Carla says things right back to me. When she does that, I know that she can hold her own. She really cares about me, and I care about her. People might not think so if they heard our conversations, but the real truth is that we do really like each other.

I had started college as a journalism major. I took several classes in that field. The classes were online, but the professors knew I had autism and typed slowly. This one class required that I attend one Saturday morning class to learn how to use the computer for the assignments. The professor saw me, and I think that ended my goal of a journalism degree. He, like many others before him, saw a drooling young man who was retarded. The hope ended because the journalism department questioned whether I was really the one typing. They decided that they would not waive a class that required me to use a camera. I cannot physically manipulate a camera due to my motor control problems.

The first obstacle in earning my journalism degree had been taking a foreign language class. Carla had solved that problem by finding

an online Spanish class. We did it during the summer. However, the camera class could not or would not be waived or adapted for me. I believe they had doubts about my ability. Consequently, I am majoring in General Studies with a psychology minor.

Carla and I have been together four years now. Having been through different facilitators, I am glad that she is staying with me. I hate thinking that someday I might have to find someone else, but I think God will help me when the time comes. He takes care of me.

Carla has started her fifth year with Matthew. She is another answer to a huge prayer. It almost seems like God lets us flounder and struggle for a while so we learn to sincerely appreciate the right person when she comes along. She has worked so hard with Matthew to be a good facilitator so that he gets to say what he wants to say. She is more than a good facilitator. She has become not only Matt's friend, but a friend to our family. As all of Matthew's facilitators have done since he started college, Carla comes to our house each day to take Matt to class and to work with him on his assignments. When you see someone every day, that person becomes a part of your family's life. She has shared our family's struggles and triumphs. She has become a member of our family in many respects.

Even though Matt has a skilled and dedicated facilitator, he continues to have good and bad days. He has days full of behavior issues where he refuses to type. Other days he will be the super student. The why is often still a mystery. Sometimes he will later tell me what's going on, but often he doesn't, (or can't perhaps), share what is causing these bad days. Other times he knows the reason but just waits a while before sharing what is going on in his mind.

This past January we found out that he had achieved enough hours to be considered a senior. Mel and I congratulated him, shared the news with others, and generally made a big deal of it. A month later he took his first test in his Criminal Justice class and got an F. Carla said he just refused to type much, or any, on some of the questions. She knew that he understood the material and could have answered the question, but he chose not to. The same thing happened on the second test. If most students fail a class, they can just take it over again with only a financial loss. However, Matt's case is totally different. Vocational Rehabilitation pays for his facilitator to attend classes and work with him for thirty-seven hours every week. If his G.P.A. gets below a 2.0 any semester, the funding will stop. Matt's grade point average was 3.5, but I knew that with just one bad semester, the facilitator and everything would be gone. The only recourse would be for us to pay the salary of a facilitator, and that would be nearly impossible for us to do.

Finally after two months of asking Matt why he was not trying on the tests, he typed that he did not want to graduate. Being a senior meant that he was close to graduation. He further explained that he was scared and typed, "School is all I have known." Many times there are underlying thoughts in his brain, as is the case with all of us. Sometimes I find out what they are, and sometimes I never know. Needless to say, it can be a very frustrating thing. Even though Matthew types, there often remains a huge wall between us. As I have said before, I just want to tear down that wall and say, "Talk to me! Verbally talk to me!" I only wish he could. That's one thing I will look forward to in heaven someday – a nice, long verbal conversation with my son.

CHAPTER 26

Plans for My Future

I think that someday I would love to have my own house to live in. I realize that I would need someone to help me take care of myself. I hope that someday I will be able to support myself. I want to write for my career. I wanted to do journalism, but for now that has been put on hold. However, I don't have to have the degree in order to write for myself. I hope to be able to freelance write for magazines and newspapers. This past year I got to interview an Amish family. It was an assignment to spend a couple of hours in a different culture. My uncle arranged the interview with a family who he knew from his dairy business. Since the woman

had a brother with autism, her family agreed to let me come to their home. I was so grateful they let me have that experience.

I mainly want to let others, like myself, know that there is hope. I have thought so many times about how Helen Keller lived in the dark and silent world with only her sense of smell, taste, and touch. She had no way to communicate to the world. Fortunately, she had a family who loved her and searched for a way to reach her. She was so lucky to have had determined parents as well as a persistent teacher who discovered the intelligence within her.

I think the greatest thing that I can do with my life is to help parents see that you have to have faith that God will help you do your best to support your child. I know that parents sometimes have fears about their disabled child. They do not want people in society to hurt their child by staring or making comments, so they try protecting them by keeping them home. I used to think I was not as good as normal people, but now I know I am. I just am different. I have some purpose. God has a reason for my life.

The plan for my life is to help the parents with children with special needs. I hope they read this book and find hope. Good parents want their children to meet their potential no matter what it is. Having a child who is

disabled should not change that. Parents must remain determined to find the means that will help their child reach that potential. It is not easy, and there will be obstacles. This cannot hinder the parents. They have to keep looking for ways to overcome those obstacles.

I hope that teachers and school administrators will have the attitude that disabled children can achieve lots of things. "Special needs" does not mean retarded; it just means that students may not do the same work as others or be able to show their skills in the usual way. They deserve understanding and respect from the school system. I hope that reading the story of my experiences will help the school systems to realize that there are those students who do not look or act like most kids, but that doesn't mean they don't belong there in the classroom with everyone else. The maximum amount of knowledge a person has cannot always be determined by outward appearance. If it was, the story of my life so far would be a very different one.

I wish I could write "and they lived happily ever after" at the end of this book, but that's just not the way it is. Finding Matthew "in there" and knowing he could understand, think, feel, and learn was truly a miracle in itself. I often wonder how many men and women with autism have gone to their graves undiscovered. It breaks my heart to think of others who may now be in the same situation Matthew was in, without anyone knowing that they did understand spoken words and what was going on in the world around them. Just because these people don't act like they understand certainly doesn't mean that they don't.

I'll never forget that summer when we discovered that Matthew could facilitate. I ran into a friend of mine who also had a son with autism. The boys had been in the same kindergarten class. I excitedly told her our story. Her first comment was, "*Matthew* did this?" My first reaction was to feel hurt, but I realized exactly what she meant – I would have never believed it either if I hadn't lived through the experience that summer.

Matthew's life changed dramatically because of facilitated communication. However, it has not been the magic cure for his autism. I can't say, in any way, that he has been cured. He is not "normal." Matthew still is very autistic. He rocks, he drools, and he plays with a toy that he enjoys, repetitively pushing the same buttons. To see him in a grocery store or anywhere in public, he appears mentally handicapped, and in many respects he is. But as you sit and watch the words that can pour out of his finger, through facilitated communication, he is far from below average in intelligence.

I often lay awake at night and wonder what will happen to Matthew; what will happen to him when Mel and I are gone? I know he has loving, devoted siblings, but they will also have their own lives and families. He has a wonderful mind, but what will he be able to do with it? My dream is that he will someday be able to type independently and not have to depend on a facilitator. Right now, however, that is not the case. Just as we have done for the last twenty-seven years, we are going to take one day at a time, planning ahead the best that we can, but we also will continue to pray and watch where God leads Matthew. Matt's dream was to write this book and to make sure that parents, families, and teachers of special needs children do not give up on them. I joined him on his mission. Hopefully, if you are reading this now, his dream has been accomplished.

Conclusion

One day I was watching a news program that featured parents of handicapped children, particularly children with autism, talking about their sons or daughters and their experiences. Many of the parents said that if they could change their children into "normal" children, they would not choose to do so.

I, on the other hand, feel much differently. I don't think I would change Matthew for my own sake, although there are probably days I might. I would, however, change him for his sake. I know how much he has missed and is still missing. I would let him change in a heartbeat if God gave us that choice. I have never asked him what he would choose, because as of right now, that has never been an option. I would love for him to have friends and the ability to communicate verbally and feed and dress himself without assistance. I can't imagine what a humbling experience it is for him to have someone help him do all of those basic tasks.

I would not change the experiences I have already had with Matthew. The bond I have formed with him is immeasurable. There is a love deep inside my heart that I cannot begin to express. Going through life with him and facing the obstacles, one after another, has made me a far better person than I could ever have been without a child with autism. It has made me realize how amazing every single birth of a normal child is. The fact that each finger and toe develops, the heart with its four chambers, each vital organ, the brain, the eyes, ears... It is truly amazing to me that so many children are born with perfect or nearly perfect minds and bodies. I also have so much more patience than I ever thought possible. I always told my mother that God gave me Matthew because I was not a patient person. I have learned that, as my mother always, told me, "You don't have to look far to find someone who is worse off that you."

As I have gone through life with Matt, there has really been no one with any definitive answers. The doctors don't know what to say or how to advise us about what to do or not to do. I don't have any close friends with a disabled child. I have met the parents of children with disabilities through Matt's schooling, but even with them, each child is so different and unique in his or her own behaviors, intelligence and obstacles.

Consequently, I found myself turning more and more to God. If I was to get any answers, I knew they would have to come from Him. I don't know if I actually have any more answers, but I have found a wealth of strength. There were days and nights when I felt things were so hopeless and out of my control. I found myself talking more and more with God. With each crisis, there are more tears and feelings of despair, but eventually, the light appears at the end of the tunnel – every time. I don't think that my faith would ever have been this deep without Matthew in my life.

I hope that teachers and all adults will understand that there is often so much more beneath the surface of what we see. No one should underestimate the abilities that may lie within. Matthew hates being talked down to. It happens so frequently. People are not intentionally trying to be hurtful, but they just don't understand that even adults with disabilities want to be spoken to as adults. Matthew gives the outer appearance of understanding very little. He does not physically respond to people's commands or requests, but he does understand every word that is being spoken. He is very aware of being spoken to as if he were a child, and he is also aware of being ignored as if he is not even present.

If I could change things for him now, I would. I feel like I have cheated Matthew out of the life he should have had. I know it is probably not anything I did, but he was conceived and developed in my body. He is an amazing person. If I could give him the rest of his life as a normal adult, I would. I can't imagine what he would be able to do with his life after the experiences he has had. He would truly be a gift to the world. As it is, I think Matthew is already a gift, not only to me, but to all the other people his life has touched.

Matthew, Mel, and I have all been blessed with a very supportive family and friends. They have done so much to help us. I hope, as a result of knowing Matthew, they, too, have gained something from the experience. Mel and I see how much our other children's lives have been affected by growing up with Matt. Both Joey and Katy used to come to me at different times, crying and say, "Mommy, what's going to happen to Matthew some day?" They both have shown Matthew so much love. Our experiences living with Matt have made them more accepting and understanding of people with disabilities. Joey is now a doctor specializing in pediatric critical care. Katy is teaching developmental preschool to three and four year-olds with special needs. Mel had at one time resigned from his fifth grade teaching position to go to work for himself, and now he teaches middle school working with severely disabled students. The three of them are all excellent at what they do and work with passion in their chosen careers. Matthew, being who he is, has affected their lives.

I only hope this book will also touch others' lives, but especially those who need it the most – those parents and families just starting their own lives with their special children.

My greatest hope is that just one other family will read this book to get the message that facilitated communication does work for some people. I think that God wants me to share my experiences for that purpose. My life and desires would be so different without it. I want to thank those people who have believed the fact that I am in here.

About the Authors

Matt Hobson currently studies at Indiana University Purdue University of Indianapolis. He plans to receive his college degree in May 2011. Matt is majoring in General Studies with a minor in Psychology, He hopes to pursue a career in journalism. Nancy Hobson has taught elementary school for 37 years in Brownsburg, Indiana. Matt and Nancy both like to travel and spend time with family. They especially enjoy going to Captiva Island, Florida for family vacations. Matt resides in Indiana with his parents, Mel and Nancy.